SMILE

FIONA BUNDELL

DEDICATION

To my much-loved husband, Peter, the kindest person I know who has faced numerous life-threatening illnesses with enduring courage and good humour.

Thank you for the love and laughter we have shared over the years.

ACKNOWLEDGMENT

My husband, Peter, who readers will come to know as DB, is owed my deepest thanks. He has read many of these anecdotes in draft form with patience and encouragement. His good humour and his unerring capacity to laugh at himself have allowed me to place him at the centre of this book.

Grateful thanks are also due to my many friends who have cajoled me for years to collect these stories into book form, to take the plunge and have them published. Thank you for all your positive comments and your belief in me.

And, of course, a huge thank you to my publishing team, who helped me prepare this book for public consumption!

CONTENTS

ABOUT THE AUTHOR

Fiona Bundell was born in Glasgow and was educated at the University of Glasgow and the Royal Scottish Academy of Music and Drama, now named the Royal Conservatoire of Scotland.

After marrying, she moved to Kent, an area known as the beautiful Garden of England, where she lives in a small village close to a river, surrounded by orchards and Oast houses.

She taught Drama, Theatre Studies, and English for thirty-five years, mainly at a Girls' Grammar School in Bexley, London, where she held the positions of Head of Year and Head of Department.

She is married to Peter, is a mother to Craig, and is an adoring grandma to Zach, Toby, and Isla.

Fiona loves theatre, acting, singing, and writing and has led several Creative Writing Workshops. This is her second book, the first one being a compilation of stories she wrote for her grandchildren. She has had an article published in 'The Times' newspaper, and one of her short stories, 'Curtain Up!' won first place in a regional writing competition, while another, 'Just a Spoonful of Sugar' won Highly Commended in a national writing competition.

INTRODUCTION

There is a well-known saying: 'Every time you find some humour in a situation, you win.' I have always tried to live by that maxim, even when life is tough. Of course, there are times for everyone when it is impossible, but when you can, the power of humour can help us to cope with life's problems.

I decided to share this philosophy with my friends and family by writing some amusing anecdotes on Facebook just to make them smile. My long-suffering husband, Peter, aka DB (Dearly Beloved), provided much of the material, principally due to his infinite gift for embroiling us in silly situations. (To be fair, I have also had my moments!)

Despite this, I love him deeply, even if his frequent role in our marriage of almost fifty years is to ensure that life doesn't run smoothly. Indeed, Murphy's Law: 'Anything that can go wrong, will go wrong' should be renamed—DB's Law. To deal with this, my choice was threefold: kill him, divorce him, or write an amusing story about it! I chose the latter.

To begin with, the stories principally dealt with mishaps that took place when we were on holiday. However, during lockdown, they obviously had to focus on more domestic events. In the hope that the stories would provide some light relief in an otherwise grim situation, a friend suggested that I call them S.M.I.L.E.—Stories Make Isolation Less Excruciating. The name stuck. After lockdown, the anecdotes focused more on the humorous little things in everyday life, and so the title became simply 'SMILE.'

Friends and family seemed to like the tales, and thus began the exhortations to collect them together into a book.

So here they are. I hope they will brighten the day of anyone who reads them, and to those who have urged me to write this book, remember that well-known saying, 'Be careful what you wish for.' You've only got yourselves to blame!

HAVE SUITCASE, WILL TRAVEL

A CAST IRON EXCUSE FOR SHOPPING!

We're enjoying a couple of days at Ironbridge—the birthplace of cast iron.

Yeah, it's not exactly top of my bucket list either, but as my Dearly Beloved studied Industrial History, he's like a kid in a candy shop.

I'd rather be soaking up the beauty of the surroundings, but DB is revelling in industrial things such as blast furnaces, ingots, and pig iron. Scintillating, eh?

Unsurprisingly, I've largely let him get on with it, but there are only so many gift shops a girl can frequent. I have just glazed over at yet another exhibition of all things iron when suddenly he catches my attention by loudly exclaiming,

'Look at that slag!'

'You can't say that!' I hiss, waiting for him to be decked by the nearby burly blond, who's been poured into some skintight, shocking-pink lycra.

'Don't be silly. It's the waste product from a blast furnace,' he explains.

'Right,' I say, rather disappointed, as the prospect of some fisticuffs might relieve the tedium of inspecting more iron ore.

Seeing an opportunity to enlighten me further, he takes the time to painstakingly explain some other iron manufacturing terms.

'Puddling' seemingly has nothing to do with OAP incontinence.

'Smelting' isn't something a frustrated Mary Berry screams when icing a chocolate cake in hot weather.

'Hematite' is not a painful ailment requiring a generous supply of Anusol.

Who knew?

Fearing that the next (excuse the pun) RIVETING activity that DB has in mind is probably a conducted tour of a Foundry or signing up for a course entitled Build Your Own Bloomery (don't ask, but old ladies' underwear doesn't come into it), I go in desperate search of another gift shop.

Somewhere! Anywhere! Please!

A TOUR DE FORCE

We're embarking on a road trip to St Maxime in the South of France. Everything has been meticulously planned and researched by moi, so what can possibly go wrong?

We arrive at our first prebooked hotel stopover and discover that Trip Advisor reviews are the stuff of fantasy! What was described as a modest hotel, perfectly adequate for a one-night stopover, turns out to be merely one step up from The Overlook, the hotel featured in the Stephen King horror film, 'The Shining.'

Monsieur Dumont, the receptionist, has a maniacal glint in his eye that would rival Jack Nicholson's in the aforementioned film, so mindful of the room in The Overlook where mayhem took place, I whisper to DB out of the side of my mouth, 'If our room number is 237, run like stink!'

As it happens, the film's Room 237 might have been the better option. The room decor is a suicidal study in maroon and brown, the bed has an ominous dip in the middle, and the ensuite has a distinct whiff of Parisian sewer.

However, a thorough check confirms there's not a blood spatter in sight, and as we're shattered after driving for hours in the rain, we decide to turn in.

It takes me a while to fall asleep, what with checking the lock on the door every five minutes and listening out for two sets of footsteps accompanied by the spine-chilling words, 'Come and play with us.' (Fans of the film will know!) But eventually, I drop off.

Soon, I'm shaken awake by DB. 'I can't get to sleep. There's a mozzie in the room. I can hear it,' he hisses, sitting bolt upright in bed.

'Is there any sign of a mad axe-wielding caretaker as well?' I ask.

'What? No!' DB says as if I'd taken leave of my senses.

'Then everything's good,' I say, burying my head under the covers again.

'No, listen!' he insists.

I listen. Nothing. Nada.

'It's gone,' I say dismissively and settle down again.

'There it is!' he shakes me awake again. 'Can't you hear it buzzing? It's going to eat me alive all night, I know it.'

I listen. Still nothing.

'There's nothing there! Now go to sleep,' I grumble and settle down again.

Just as I'm drifting off, the top sheet suddenly disappears as DB wraps himself in it from head to toe like a huge white protective cocoon.

'Oi! That's my bit of the sheet!' I protest.

'Yes, well, you don't get bitten by the little blighters like I do,' DB's muffled voice says from under the sheet.

Soon, the sound of deep breathing signals he's peacefully asleep.

Meanwhile, I lie there. Wide awake. Sheetless. Brain working overtime.

Did I just hear a subhuman cackle? Was that a menacing voice intoning, 'Here's Johnny!'

That's the thought that does it. Any chance of sleep is now gone. Meanwhile, some raucous snoring emanating from the depths of DB's chrysalis tells me that the thought of being murdered in our beds isn't keeping HIM awake!

***

DB and I eventually reach St Maxime, our final destination. The villa looks lovely, and we park the car to begin unpacking and settling in.

Now, number one son, Craig, has just bought a brand spanking new Volvo XC90 and is shortly due to arrive in it with the rest of the family in tow.

'Do you think you've left enough room for Craig's car?' I say doubtfully.

'Yes, it'll be fine,' says DB, who's desperate to have a cuppa.

'Are you sure?' I say. 'It's a bloomin' enormous thing; probably best to move ours,' I say—not wanting to nag, of course.

'All right, all right,' DB says somewhat disgruntled. 'If you insist.'

He gets back into the car and parks it closer to the villa wall.

'Will that suit your ladyship?' he says, a tad sarcastically in my estimation, and heads off for his cup of tea.

'I just thought it might be better to reverse it in,' I say nonchalantly.

'Look, I've just driven 170 miles, and all I want is a cup of tea. Is that too much for a man to ask?'

'It's just that it'll be easier to drive out, that's all.'

I use my best winsome smile.

'Ok. I give in, I'll reverse the car in and then I want a CUP OF TEA!'

'Your wish is my command,' I say sweetly.

I'm in the kitchen on the hunt for a kettle when I hear a sickening crunch.

Oh dear, I think. That doesn't sound good.

DB returns, puce in the face.

'Gosh, look at your face. You've really caught the sun,' I say as a diversionary tactic.

'I—HAVE JUST—BACKED THE AUDI—INTO A RUDDY DRAINAGE DITCH,' he says, seething. 'Goodness knows what damage it's done to the undercarriage.'

'What did you do that for?' I ask.

'It wasn't through choice,' he says through gritted teeth. 'If I'd left it where it was, it wouldn't have happened! Now, for the final time, is there any chance of that cup of tea!'

Is this a good time to tell him there isn't a kettle?

***

The family having arrived, the next day, we spend time with our three grandchildren, aka The Three Desperados.

'Come on, Grandpa, we're going to the beach today!' says Middle Desperado.

'Really? Good, oh,' says DB, the sand hater, with zero enthusiasm.

We soon arrive at a pretty beach, accompanied by much grumbling from Grandpa, or should that be Grumpa, about sand in shoes, treacherous rocks, no shade, and most importantly, lack of toilets.

We unpack everything and settle down to enjoy the sun.

'Are you sure there isn't a toilet here?' asks DB, surveying the toilet-free scene.

'No,' I say. 'And I'm up to your tricks, so no sloping off for two hours on the hunt for a loo just to get out of sitting on the beach!'

DB looks disgruntled.

'Just asking,' he says. 'It's just that I'd be comfier if there WAS a toilet, that's all.'

Five minutes later.

'How long do you think we'll be here?' asks DB.

'Most of the morning,' I say breezily and continue playing with the children.

'Humph!' says DB.

'Let's play I Spy,' suggests Oldest Desperado. 'I spy with my little eye something beginning with S.'

DB sighs.

A long wait ensues.

'Come on, Grandpa, it's your turn to guess,' says Oldest Desperado.

'What was the letter again?' asks DB.

'Oh, Grandpa!' chorus the Three Desperadoes in despair.

'Well, I'd be able to concentrate better if I knew there was a toilet,' justifies DB.

Knowing it's futile waiting for Grumpa to concentrate, I say, 'Ok, I'll guess.'

I spot the plastic toy watering can that Youngest Desperado has been playing with.

'I spy with my little eye something beginning with W.C.'

'W.C? Is there? Really? Where?' says DB, who suddenly perks up no end.

'Not that kind of W.C., for goodness' sake!' I say.

'I don't think Grandpa's got the hang of this game,' says Oldest Desperado.

Those of us without a toilet obsession carry on playing happily, interspersed with muttered comments from Grandpa:

'I got my hopes up then...'

'I'd give my eye teeth for a proper W.C...'

'One toilet, that would do...'

It's going to be a long day!

***

We've had a fabulous holiday with the family, but sadly, it's time to say, 'Au revoir, France!'

We're well into the first leg of our journey home, and DB has seriously fallen out with Doris, the sat nav lady. She is taking great enjoyment in teasing us with a series of cryptic announcements.

'An object has been reported on the road.' Doris says.

'OK,' says DB, 'but what kind of object?'

I offer some possibilities. A couple of cases of Beaujolais? A wayward baguette? Un grand fromage? DB is not amused.

'An incident has been reported ahead.' Doris continues.

'What incident, for Pete's sake!' DB mutters. 'Mind you, if these flaming French drivers keep cutting me up left, right, and centre,' he grumbles, 'the incident's going to be an Englishman punching a Frenchman's lights out!'

Just to lighten things up a little, I say, 'Probably an Onion Johnny strangled by a rebellious string of onions!' DB is still not amused.

'Twenty minutes has been added to your journey,' Doris intones.

'WHY? WHAT FOR?' yells DB, convinced Doris has got it in for him.

And to make DB's day, Doris is leading us through the centre of Lyons—the hellhole, which is a total traffic nightmare. 'What kind of road traffic planners think it's helpful to have two major highways merge together in the centre of a city!' rages DB. 'We could crawl through Lyons on our hands and knees quicker than this!'

11

Anyway, safe to say DB is more than a little « irrité » as the French say. His face hasn't been this puce since his 'contretemps' with the drainage ditch!

***

We go to check out of our hotel this morning, ready to start our final leg of the journey home. DB, whose grasp of the French language covers 'oui' 'non,' and, if he's pushed, 'la plume de ma tante,' is asked to sign the bill for the previous night's dinner. Slightly flustered at the barrage of French directed his way, he mutters 'Oui' and hurriedly signs in a bid to escape before he has to 'parlez' anything else. It is a bit of 'bonne chance' that, as the receptionist is about to put the bill into the till, I notice it totals 224 euros! Now, as we know, DB has a healthy appetite, but not even he can eat the equivalent of almost £224 of food in one sitting. Either the exchange rate has plummeted lower than a builder's bum, or there has been a mistake.

'Excusez-moi, Monsieur,' I hurriedly say and explain that this can't be our bill. There is a lot of 'Zut alors!' and a possible 'Merde!' or two before the bill is rectified.

'Imagine not checking something like that carefully,' I chastise DB. He takes the Fifth Amendment and says nothing.

Later that day, we arrive at our next hotel, which I'd booked online. 'We've booked a room for tonight,' I say in my best French. 'The name is Bundell.'

The receptionist looks at me blankly. I polish up the accent a bit and try again. She's still looking blank. She checks our names again.

'Your reservation was for last night, Madame. I'm afraid you have been charged for it, and we have no rooms available for this evening.'

Aargh! Quelle erreur!

DB can't resist a smug smile. 'What was it you said about checking everything carefully?' he says with barely disguised glee.

We manage to find another hotel, but it's in the centre of Reims and costs twice as much as the one we had previously booked. I'm in shock. There's only one thing for it—retail therapy! That'll wipe the smug look off DB's face.

A VIRGINIA ROAD TRIP

Having thoroughly enjoyed our previous American Road Trips, we decide, or should I say DB decides, that a similar trip to Virginia would be the very thing. Why Virginia? Because it is steeped in history about the American War of Independence, and just to top it off, the American Civil War too. Having failed A Level History miserably back in the day, you can imagine that I am totally thrilled about the prospect, but DB's degree is in Economic History, so he's well up for it. Plane tickets booked, we set off on the world's longest History lesson. Yay.

After grabbing the hire car at the airport, we stop at our first hotel and, to get a flavour of the place (excuse the pun), eat at the local diner. DB, who has devoured his own body weight in deep-fried mozzarella sticks and shrimp pasta, is already regretting his rash decision to pass on the pud, so decides to pop into the 7-Eleven on the way back to the hotel for a little 'something sweet'. I decide to carry on.

In the gathering dusk, what seems to me to be a fairly respectable-looking young man approaches me and says politely, 'Excuse me ma'am, do you have a dollar or two?'

Now, being completely Mutt and Jeff in one ear and not yet used to the Virginian drawl, I don't catch this.

'Sorry?' I say.

'I just wondered, ma'am, if you had a dollar or two,' he drawls again.

Nope, still can't get it.

'A dalatoo?' I say questioningly.

'Yes, ma'am,' he says.

'A dalatoo?' I say to myself. 'What the heck is that? Some sort of North American parakeet? A new kind of body art?'

'A dalatoo,' I confirm.

'Yes, ma'am,' he says, losing the will to live.

'No, sorry, I don't know what that is. What is it like?'

He looks at me with growing regret in his eyes as he realises he's dealing with some mad British eccentric.

'Don't worry, ma'am. Have a nice evening,' he says as he quickly legs it across the car park.

DB, who has now caught up with me, says with alarm, 'What the heck are you doing?'

'Well, I couldn't understand what that nice chap wanted,' I explain.

'Nice chap?' thunders DB. 'He's a panhandler! (American for street beggar, seemingly) He wan-ted a doll-lar- or- two,' he says, articulating slowly.

'Oh,' I say. 'Well, why didn't he say so?'

DB shakes his head despairingly and drags me back to the hotel.

So, tip of the week? Next time someone bothers you for money, crack on you're deaf! It works a treat!

***

I know it's going to be a bad day when one of those stupid little bars of soap you get in hotel bathrooms slips out of my hands, skitters across the sink, and drops down the toilet. DB, who still needs to shower, is not amused!

'What's the plan today?' I ask as a quick diversionary tactic. As this is an American history trip (yawn), DB is in charge of the itinerary.

'Staunton today, the birthplace of Woodrow Wilson,' says DB with glee.

'Oh. Great,' I say.

DB, sensing a certain lack of enthusiasm, quickly reassures me that it has lots of quaint shops, too.

The words 'carrot' and 'stick' come to mind.

We decide to take the tourist trolley round town. The driver, who is 80 if he's a day, proudly tells us he's a veteran (probably of the Civil War, by the looks of him). After taking three goes to climb up the front steps of the trolley with much huffing and puffing on every step, he emits a prolonged, agonised groan as he lowers himself into the seat. Once settled, he finally starts the commentary, or at least what we can hear of it, through some ill-fitting false teeth and an enormous plug of chewing tobacco.

To crown it all, we've hardly sat down, read the trolley map, and looked out of the window when we're back at the terminus! You've heard of small-town America? Well, Staunton is firmly in that league!!

Never mind, I think, we can have a look around the shops. Wrong. The music shop is shut; the deli is shut; the general store is shut; the book shop is shut. It seems all of ruddy Staunton is shut. Main Street is like a ghost town. In fact, a few ghosts might have livened the place up a bit!

'Oh well, there's always Walmart,' says DB as a way of consolation. 'Probably get a decent bar of soap there!'

***

Tonight, DB tried to kill me.

We took a guided tour round Monticello today, home of Thomas Jefferson. The tour takes about 3 to 4 hours in total, so we are footsore and weary by the end of the day. The snag is that our hotel is on the outskirts of town, which means there is no restaurant nearby.

We decide to eat in our room. Trying to avoid the clogged arteries that a fast-food outlet would ensure, we opt for a trip to the local supermarket. I decide on a tuna salad. Buy some salad; open a tin of tuna; job done. One small problem. A tin of tuna requires a tin opener, right?

DB sympathises briefly but then decides his arteries can stand a bit more clogging and goes off to search for something more tasty for himself. A few minutes later, he returns triumphant.

'Guess who's found you a tin of tuna with a ring pull!' he announces with a self-satisfied smile.

'Well done!' I say gratefully as he throws it in the basket with the other items, and we head off for the checkout.

Back at the hotel, I'm about to open the tuna when I see something that stops me in my tracks.

A picture.

Of a cat.

A cat?

Yep. A cat.

DB's ring pull tin of tuna, which he so carefully found for me, is, in fact, cat food!

The fact it is <u>prime</u> cat food, as DB points out, does not make it any better in my book. Nor the fact that the cat looks cute!

It is cat food.

I nearly ate it.

DB swore it was an honest mistake. I swore, too.

***

DB and I decide to spend some time on the ocean wave today, fulfilling one of DB's dreams—sailing on a fully rigged schooner.

His eyes light up as we board the ship. It's not long before the crew are persuading the passengers to get involved in the full sailing ship experience. Before you can say 'Roger the cabin boy,' DB is channelling his inner pirate and volunteering to hoist the mainsail or whatever it's called. Is that wise, I think? This is DB. DB of complex cardiac problems too numerous to mention!

'I don't think that's a good idea,' I say.

No response.

'I REALLY don't think that's a good idea,' I repeat as DB's face takes on a worrying reddish hue. The young slip of a girl who is one of the crew doesn't make it any better when she tells us, 'This gentleman is hoisting the heaviest sail of them all.' Great, I think, wondering if there's any way we can sail this thing straight into the nearest A and E.

At last, the sail is hoisted. DB is gasping but happy, and my nerves are in shreds. I wonder what other crazy seafaring activities DB is going to volunteer for. Manning the crow's nest? Swabbing the decks? Walking the plank? Anyway, it's all worth it. DB is a very happy bunny (or whatever the nautical equivalent is. A very happy haddock?). Admittedly, he's more Captain Pugwash than Jack Sparrow (shame), but he's *my* Captain Pugwash. All I have to do now is stop him from buying an eye patch in the gift shop!

***

We set sail again today, but this time on a cruiser down the Potomac River to Washington, DC. DB is clearly missing his pirate role of yesterday so I'm preparing to rugby tackle him if he dares suggest lifting the anchor. After chatting to a fellow passenger, however, his eyes light up again. Never a good sign.

'Look!' he says, pointing to a huge building with a radar system that looks like giant golf balls on the roof. 'It's Langley, the centre for the CIA.'

'What?' I say.

'Langley. Carrie Mathison? Sergeant Brody?'

I'm still looking blank.

'Homeland. The TV series. We watched it.'

'Oh yes.' The penny finally drops.

'That building is Langley, where all the CIA agents hang out. Exciting, isn't it!'

DB dons his dark glasses—to look more the part—as he transports himself into the realms of espionage and secret surveillance. Goodbye, Captain Pugwash; hello, Jason

Bourne. He's just mentally polishing up some killer assassin moves when his bubble is cruelly 'burst.'

The same passenger who'd told him it was Langley admits he's unwittingly given us duff info. The building is, in fact, the Washington Naval Research Laboratory—still pretty secret but definitely not in the same league as CIA Headquarters!

DB's little face falls. He takes off his dark glasses. His fantasy role as a CIA agent is over. Perhaps being a pirate is exciting enough, after all.

A few minutes later, I catch him enthusiastically sizing up some heavy ropes coiled up on deck. That rugby tackle is still on the cards!

***

Today it is raining.

Again.

But being intrepid Britishers, we brave the wind and rain and set off for Mount Vernon, George Washington's gaff. A tour round his house will also hopefully keep us warm and dry. How wrong we are!

Now, can you imagine what ex-teachers dread most when going around a historic building? Yep, a coach load of school kids. And not just one, not just two, but THREE coach loads of the little blighters arrive just ahead of us in the car park. We try to outrun them, but it isn't easy, what with DB and his dodgy toe (don't ask—but 'ingrown' and 'toenail' might give you a clue), so we find ourselves waiting—in the rain—at the back of an ENORMOUS queue. Did I mention it is raining?

'Never mind,' says DB cheerfully, 'There's a film in the visitors' centre about Washington's first military victory. It should be fascinating.'

I look at him long and hard.

'Really?' I say.

'And it'll be warm and dry in there,' DB adds cleverly.

Now, normally, I'd rather poke my eye out with a sharp stick than watch a film about military action, but being cold, wet, and miserable, even I begin to think it's appealing.

We settle ourselves in the film theatre to discover it's interactive—one of those cinemas where you physically experience what's happening on the screen as you watch it.

'Washington's men fell under heavy artillery fire.'

Boom! We feel the seats shake under us.

'Gunfire filled the air with smoke. '

Smoke is pumped out from behind the screen.

Then come the fateful words.

'They marched through a terrible snowstorm for nine long miles.'

Yep, you've guessed it.

Snow—and I mean real snow—begins to fall on the audience. Just as we've begun to dry out, we're soaking wet again!

That does it for me. I give DB one of my best 'disgruntled wife' looks and march off in search of the cafeteria to find a nice hot cup of tea.

But I forgot; this is America.

A lukewarm one is the best I can hope for.

***

Well, our holiday is at an end, and it's safe to say I'm totally Museum-ed out!

We've spent three weeks exploring the American War of Independence and the Civil War, which, as a compete non-historian, I've frequently mixed up, reducing poor DB to near apoplexy! But I've learned a huge amount, not just about American history but also how different its culture is to ours. Here are some of the most amusing and totally genuine oddities we've seen on this trip.

1. Motorway names—nothing succinct like M25 or M6—but names of people: christian, middle, and surname! Try punching 'The Kenneth Eugene Clodfeather Highway' into your sat nav!

2. As DB found out to his cost, dispensing petrol, or gas as they call it, is much more complicated in the U.S. Strange,

really, as DB never usually has trouble dispensing gas (make of that what you will!)

3. TV adverts for prescription drugs, which terrify the living daylights out of you! We've heard ads where the possible side effects have been 'may cause suicidal tendencies' or 'danger of severe anaphylactic shock'!

4. Coffee shops with so many options of Frappalatte, Crappacino, Espressiato, or whatever they're called, and the palaver involved in making them, it's lunchtime before you've ordered your morning coffee!

5. Notice at the side of the highway: 'SPEED LIMIT ENFORCED BY AIRCRAFT' How? By dropping a cluster bomb on offenders? And you thought a speeding ticket was bad!

And the final one...

6. Shops with such incongruous names that you think twice before shopping there! Names we saw, and I promise you I haven't made these up, are:

- RANDY'S MATTRESSES (suppose he's tested them all one way or another!)

- DUNKIN'S DIAMONDS (who'd buy diamonds from a man who can't even spell his own name correctly!)

- BURKE'S BANK (Would you put your money in the hands of a Burke?)

- KILLER COFFEE (really?)

AND THEY SAY ROMANCE IS DEAD!

We're in the New Forest for a short break, and despite the disappointing weather, we're once again amazed by its beauty.

Beaulieu is today's port of call, and DB has promised we'll go somewhere nice for lunch to make up for the cloudy conditions.

Walking through the village, I can see some pretty tearooms and a rather nice hotel, so I'm full of expectations for a lovely lunch.

As we admire the picturesque setting of the village, I decide a trip to the loo wouldn't go amiss, so I retrace my steps to the toilet, which I'd spotted earlier. While I'm gone, DB promises to suss out a place for lunch.

I eventually catch him up and ask if he's chosen our lunch venue.

'Absolutely, my precious,' he says.

My precious? My precious? Immediately, my Drivel Detector goes on red alert.

'What do you mean?' I ask suspiciously.

'Exactly what I say, oh light of my life.'

The needle on the Drivel Detector goes into overdrive.

'I've found us a charming lunch spot,' he continues as he ushers me quickly across the road. 'Nothing is too good for you, my darling.'

The needle now surges from 'piffle' to 'complete guff'.

'It's quiet, it's rustic, it has a lovely view… and it's here,' he indicates a spot before him with a flourish.

'It's a bus shelter!' I splutter.

'Ah, yes, it may look like a bus shelter…'

'That's because it IS a bus shelter!' I interrupt. 'Look at the sign. It quite clearly says BUS STOP; ergo, this is a BUS SHELTER!'

'But you haven't seen the beautiful view,' he says desperately. 'Look round here.' He disappears behind the bus shelter, beckoning me to follow him.

'You mean I'm not having lunch in a bus shelter, but in the BACK of a bus shelter! And that is supposed to be better, how?' I'm now in full rant mode.

'Well, you know what they say, "Never too old to have a thrill in the back of a bus shelter,"' he says in his best 'cheeky chappie' voice, then tapers off as he sees my face.

I reluctantly follow him to find a bench on the other side of the bus shelter, which, admittedly, looks over some water and a bit of greenery.

'See, none of your 'sarf' London bus stops here! Not an iota of graffiti in sight!' he adds triumphantly.

'There's another small problem,' I point out. 'Lunch usually means some sort of food is involved. Or do bus drivers double up as waiters in this neck of the woods?' I say in my best sarcastic tone.

'Sorted!' he says and digs into the depths of a brown paper carrier bag. 'I found a fabulous Deli in the high street, and this looked so delicious I couldn't resist it!'

Things are looking up! Something delicious from a Deli… perhaps some finely sliced prosciutto or creamy goats' cheese or tangy humus….

My mouth begins to water, and I'm just about to forgive him when, from the carrier bag, he pulls an enormous sausage roll, one the size of a small shed.

'Thought we could share it…' DB says generously.

Marvellous. My much-anticipated lunch consists of half a sausage roll in the back of a bus shelter. I can hardly contain my excitement.

AW' RIGHT BUTT!

There's nothing like a stroll along the prom for whetting your appetite. Now, it's undeniable that DB's appetite is 'healthy' at the best of times, but after a walk in the bracing sea breezes of The Gower, it's safe to say that his appetite is not so much 'whetted' as saturated!

He's very disappointed, therefore, not to say distraught, when he discovers that there's no café within staggering distance that can provide him with his favourite sweet Welsh delicacy.

'Right, I need some bara brith,' he proclaims. 'Get in the car, and we'll find that cafe at the other end of the prom.'

We find it easily and park the car.

Then, the fun begins.

As we all know, DB's war with technology is legendary, but until now has been mainly restricted to computers and mobile phones. After this morning's shenanigans, I can safely say that car parking machines have joined the ranks of insubordination.

The biggest problem is that the machine's instructions are in Welsh. There's no button that says 'translate into English' that we can see, so we struggle on, trying to decipher what appears to us to be complete gobbledygook.

Now, I love the Welsh people. They're warm and kind human beings. One of my best friends is Welsh. But does there really need to be that number of consonants in one Welsh word? REALLY? It's obvious King Gruffud, or whoever is responsible for the Welsh language, had a serious prejudice against vowels. Perhaps he had Irritable Vowel Syndrome. (Sorry, couldn't resist!) Surely, just a few sprinkled here and there wouldn't be too much to ask.

In contrast, French at least gives you a few clues that allow a decent stab at what a word means, e.g., 'numéro d'enregistrement' isn't too difficult to work out, is it? But we're faced with the words 'Rhif cofrestru'. I mean, where's the clue in that? You've got no chance of guessing what that means unless you've got a degree in hieroglyphics. Or Welsh. Welsh would help.

Anyway, after a few uneducated guesses and repeated attempts to ram a variety of coins into a slot which keeps spitting them back, it's safe to say DB is completely hacked off.

'All I wanted was a cup of tea and a slice of bara brith,' he bemoans. 'Is that too much to ask?'

'Never mind,' I say consolingly, 'We might not need one at this rate 'cos the car's probably been towed away by now!'

Hunger pangs getting the better of him, DB resorts to his usual 'cheesed off with technology' technique of frantically stabbing every button on the machine in the futile hope that something registers.

More and more incomprehensible words flash up on the screen.

'Look! Look at that! What's that supposed to mean?' he cries in disgust.

'Probably; stop pushing all my buttons like a maniac and punch in the proper thing,' I suggest.

'I tell you what I'd like to punch in. "SOD OFF YOU STUPID MACHINE!" How do you say THAT in Welsh?' he yells at the screen. 'Eh? Eh? Ha, not so clever NOW, are we!'

Seeing that DB is on the verge of going full Basil Fawlty and teaching this uncooperative machine a thing or two by giving it a good kicking, a local appears to see if he can help.

'Aw' right, butt?'

We explain the problem that the machine won't take our coins.

'Ah well, you see, it's a card-only machine, it is,' he says. 'Look, it says it there, 'Taliad cerdyn yn unig'—plain as day, mun.'

Before DB finds his 'cerdyn' and shoves it where the Welsh sun don't shine, I hastily thank the man, and with his help, we complete the transaction.

Finally, we make our way to the cafe and sit down. DB is positively drooling at the thought of the bara brith he's been dreaming about for the past few hours.

'What can I get for you?' asks the waitress.

'I'd like some tea and a slice of your best bara brith,' says DB, good humour restored.

'Aw, sorry, cariad, it's lunches only now, it is!'

DB is speechless. In fact, in true Welsh parlance, he's absolutely tampin', he is!

BATH TIME

So, DB and I are in Bath. Not THE bath—that would be weird—Bath, in Somerset. We're taking an open-top bus trip around the city. I'm optimistic that the weather is going to be warm and dress appropriately. I soon find out that the early morning sun is having a laugh because it's bloomin' freezing! We arrive at the bus stop early, so a trip to the nearby M and S vest department for an extra layer seems a good idea. Peter protests.

'We'll miss the bus.'

'No, we won't, we're early.'

'We didn't come all the way to Bath, one of the most beautiful cities in England, to go to Marks and Spencer's,' he fumes.

'Won't be a mo,' I assure him breezily.

'Heard that one before,' he mutters.

The undies' department is at the far end of the shop, which naturally necessitates walking through all the other departments.

'Ooh, that's nice.

Wonder if they've got this in another colour?

Like the look of that.

Does this suit me?'

Needless to say, it takes a while for me to get the vest top I went in for, find the changing room, and don said garment.

When we eventually arrive at the bus stop, we're just in time to see the back of the bus disappear into the distance.

DB is not best pleased.

Standing at the bus stop, a cool breeze blows up.

'Ooh, that wind's chilly, ' I say. 'Do you think I could get a scarf somewhere?'

Seeing the thunderous look in my husband's eye, I decide to forgo the scarf, lest it become a murder weapon.

The second day of our Bath visit dawns bright and sunny.

'Ha, I'm not falling for that one again,' I think as I pull on my trusty vest of yesterday and, just to be on the safe side, a thicker jumper.

By the afternoon, the sun is blazing, and I'm getting hotter and hotter. Not daring to even hint at visiting M and S again for a cooling t-shirt, I suffer in silence.

By the afternoon, I'm beyond 'glowing,' as my mother insisted ladies do when they're hot. What to do? Should I risk arrest by trying out the Roman baths for real? But then the water is 46C—not much good when you already resemble a menopausal lobster.

So, we retire to the Pump Room—Bath's answer to Palm Court—for some refreshing afternoon tea. Realising that ditching the jumper and sitting in my vest might not go down too well in this genteel tearoom, I rely on the air conditioning to come to my rescue.

'You're looking a tad hot,' DB, the master of understatement, declares as he sees my sweat-beaded brow. 'How about a glass of bath water?' he suggests.

'Uuurgh, disgusting!' I say until he explains, he means Bath water and not bath water!

BON VOYAGE!

Ooh, la, la! We're off to La Riviera for a week. Living the life of jet setters, you might think, however, disavow yourself immediately of that idea because we're travelling Ryanair. Ryanair doesn't do jets. More giant air-fix kits and a bumper pack of elastic bands.

DB has circumvented Ryanair's ridiculous baggage restrictions by dressing like a walking wardrobe—cargo pants with pockets galore bulging with extra socks and pants; a man bag—also with endless pockets—stuffed with a variety of useless junk in most people's eyes, but which to DB, are the necessities of life itself. He is so weighed down that it's safe to say that any self-respecting Mafia member would be ditching their concrete shoes and getting in a supply of DB's man bags. And, oh yes, because it won't fit in the piddly little bag they allow you, he's wearing his Panama hat. He's rocking the look of a well-stuffed, overdressed scarecrow.

We pass through security, which, of course, entails him emptying every blessed thing out into not just one tray but several, and then the whole rigmarole of stuffing everything back where it belongs starts again. By this time, the people in the queue behind us, sensing it's going to be a long night, are finding their pyjamas and toothbrushes.

At last, we get to the gate to board.

'Can I have my boarding pass?' I ask.

'Sure,' DB says and looks in a pocket in his man bag. Then, in another pocket. Then another. Then, one by one, in every pocket in his cargoes.

Need I say more? There is no boarding pass. Correction—there is ONE boarding pass, HIS boarding pass, but not mine.

'Brilliant!' I say through very gritted teeth. 'So, you're off to France, but I'm on the bus back home!'

'It must be somewhere,' he says.

'Well, obviously!' I hiss, 'but it's not here, is it!'

So, the great pocket emptying starts again. Those who had been in the queue behind us in security, begin to groan audibly. 'Not that eejit again!'

To cut a very long story short, my boarding pass is not in ANY of the hundred pockets that festoon my Dearly Beloved. I send him off to throw himself at the boarding steward's feet. Some minutes later, he returns with a scrappy bit of paper, which is only one step up from the back of a fag packet and tells me that that will get me on the plane.

I'm doubtful. However, it works. We get on the plane, settle down, and DB takes off his hat. There, snuggled safely in the crown, is my boarding pass!

'Oh, that's where I put it,' DB says with a smile of satisfaction.

I say nothing.

I have no words.

Well, maybe a few— 'Mon mari est un complete numpty!'

***

I'd like to say that the rest of the journey goes without incident, but I'd be lying.

We cross the tarmac to board the plane. Now, I'm no aeronautical engineer, but something in the engine sounds distinctly dodgy—like you've chucked a canteen of cutlery in a tumble drier.

Settling into our seats, the noise only gets louder. 'Just ignore it,' says DB, which, right now, is about as useful to me as a concrete parachute! DB snoozes his way through the flight; I spend it manically gripping the arms of my seat while running through various scenarios of impending doom.

So, I'm not exactly filled with glee when we're about to land, and the plane suddenly aborts its descent within a few hundred metres of the runway and soars vertically upwards. My gum chewing goes from leisurely to frantic in seconds. I'm within a nanosecond of voluntarily donning the full life jacket and oxygen mask combo (not to mention clean underwear) when we straighten up.

The pilot has a second go, approaching from the sea. We're so close to the waves that I can smell the dodgy trainers in Davey Jones' locker, so this is only a marginally better choice in my book.

After much fervent praying, we land successfully, then it's the long wait for the luggage.

Gradually, everyone else disperses with their bags, but, surprise, surprise, my case is still missing; presumed gone for ever.

Great.

I picture myself resorting to wearing some of DB's cast-offs, but will a voluminous T-shirt, a pair of baggy cargoes, and a ma-hussive pair of trainers cut the mustard in the upmarket marina of St Maxime? Doubtful.

Thankfully, just as I'm about to give up all hope, a lone case trundles its way around the baggage belt. It's mine. Another sigh of relief.

Does it end there? Oh no.

***

So, having survived a near-crash landing (well, in my book) and a wayward suitcase, off we go to the car hire depot. I wait outside with the luggage while DB goes inside and murders the French language at reception. Sometime later, he emerges looking red-faced and frazzled and says, for security reasons, he needs his passport.

DUN-DUN-DUN!!!!

Alarm bells ring.

I know that having just gone through the fiasco of my missing boarding pass, giving DB any other important document is a recipe (school dinner type, not Jamie Oliver) for COMPLETE disaster!' However, as I'm guarding the cases outside, I'm left with no choice.

The hire car is eventually sorted. It's late now, and we're tired and hungry, so I make DB swear that all the documentation is safe, and we set off for St Maxime, an hour and a half's drive away.

The following day, I ask DB for his passport, and..... yep, 'quelle surprise', it's missing. A search ensues. Nothing, nada, nowt, diddly squat. So, it's a choice of driving all the way back to the airport and practising, 'Pardon monsieur, mon mari est un complete lummox et a perdu son sodding passport,' or just chuck in the sponge and head straight for the British Consulate.

I hunt one last time before getting in the car. There it is, in the folder that DB has already 'searched' twice.

'Well, that's a relief,' says DB. 'I'm going for a swim in the pool.'

Hmmm, wonder if there's a job lot of piranhas for sale somewhere? Asking for a friend.

***

After this fraught start, the holiday goes relatively smoothly—well, for the Bundells, it does—granted, that doesn't set the bar very high. My birthday falls on the last day, so DB suggests we have a celebration in the evening. Being in the South of France, this may conjure up a certain image of French sophistication: an elegant dress, carefully coiffed hair, a cloud of expensive perfume. But not for this birthday girl. Oh no.

As we're dining al fresco at our villa, my outfit owes more to its mosquito-proofing properties than chic elegance: a baggy T-shirt with trousers tied at the ankles. (Those vicious little blighters get everywhere.) And the fragrant French perfume? A choking cloud of 'Eau de Deet' mozzie repellent (the smell of which is guaranteed to kill a horse at ten paces but has zero chance of making a mozzie even sneeze). And as a finishing feature, having slept with my head only inches from an electric fan all week in a bid to escape the 100-degree heat in the bedroom, I have a barnet that resembles a haystack.

DB takes one look at me and says, 'See, you've made an effort, ma cherie!'

Husbands! Zut alors!

***

Too soon, it's time to go home. DB and I arrive at Nimes airport in good time, despite the emergency stop to check that DB's case was actually in the car and not, as he initially feared, still standing on the driveway of the villa. Now, those of you who have experienced Nimes will know that, as airports go, it is only one step up from a shed with a toilet, so the plan is that an early arrival will mean fewer crowds. But no such luck. The only open check-in desk has an interminable queue, so we join it with heavy hearts, knowing it's going to be a long wait. A long, long wait. A long, long, long... ok, you get the gist.

The queue is moving at a snail's pace—and that would be a geriatric snail…with bunions…and fallen arches. And we wait and wait and wait. DB reckons he might need another shave if we have to wait much longer, but at last, we reach the check-in desk. I hand over our tickets.

'You are going to Stansted,' the girl says in a heavy French accent.

'Yes,' I say as DB loads the luggage onto the belt.

'No, Madame, you are going to Stansted,' she says again.

'Yes,' I say again.

'We cannot take your luggage,' she continues.

What? Ryanair might be a budget airline, but surely we don't have to fling our cases into the hold ourselves!

She sees my blank look.

'You are going to Stansted,' she says for the third time, sounding like a repetitive parrot, then continues,

'This is the queue for Fez.'

Our hearts plummet. We've waited all that time in the wrong queue. Realising the dilemma, DB risks a hernia by desperately dragging our cases off the luggage belt before they're whisked off to Morocco for all time.

We look round and see that, by now, a different queue has formed. One that snakes twice round the departure hall and all the way out of the airport door.

Yep. That would be the queue for Stansted.

We trundle our cases outside to join the end of the line and wonder whether it wouldn't be quicker to walk home.

To add insult to injury, we discover that our flight is delayed by an hour and a half. We had left the villa early with no breakfast, except for a small croissant and a cup of, not so much weak as positively helpless, French 'tea'. DB, who's never at his most sunny when he's hungry, is becoming more peeved with every passing minute.

We eventually board and land in the UK at 2.00 pm. DB, starving, hastily marches off to catch the shuttle bus to the off-site parking lot, intent on getting home ASAP so he can feed his grumbling stomach. A bus eventually pulls up, and we set off for the 20-minute journey to the car park.

'I'm blooming ravenous!' declares DB.

I scrabble in the bottom of my bag and offer him a mint that's past its best.

'I'm not hungry for a mint!' he says, eyeing it suspiciously. 'And certainly not THAT mint!'

I wipe off a bit of fluff and offer it again.

He looks at it disparagingly. 'I need a proper meal! I'm in danger of malnutrition here!'

(I don't point out that even if he lost several stones, he wouldn't be a candidate for malnutrition.)

'Well, it won't be long before we'll be home.' I say soothingly.

We arrive at the parking lot; I stand guard over the luggage, and DB goes into the reception to present the car park ticket.

He soon returns, looking thunderous.

'I don't BELIEVE it!' he splutters, outdoing Victor Meldrew by a mile. 'This is the wrong *#@*!!#* car park! This is Purple Parking, and we're parked in APH. We've got to get back on the bus, go back to the airport, and start again!'

I consider wringing his neck, but there are too many witnesses, so we get back on the bus.

It's now completely deserted. The driver has gone AWOL; there are no passengers. It's like the Marie Celeste of buses.

We sit and wait. Again.

'What's the driver doing?' I wonder.

'Obviously having lunch,' snarls DB, 'like every other sane person is having!' he says, his mood blackening even more.

Suddenly, a glint of hope appears in his eyes. 'I could highjack the bus, find a Subway, and then get back here before anyone notices.'

I give him one of my looks.

At last, a different driver arrives. He's a plump fellow, and for a horrible moment, I fear DB is about to turn cannibal, as he's salivating and licking his lips. But no, what he's looking at is the large ham sandwich which the driver is tucking into.

I downgrade the possibility of cannibalism to a mugging.

Sandwich polished off, the driver starts the engine and off we go back to the airport.

DB looks out of the window at the passing scene like a sulky child.

'Look, there's a Starbucks. And a KFC. And a Burger King,' his tone wistful, his nose pressed against the glass.

We sail past them all and, at last, get back to the terminal.

We get on our THIRD bus and, finally, arrive at the correct parking site, collect the car, and set off for home.

'Do you know the time?' I ask, looking at my watch. 'It's nearly four o'clock. We should skip lunch and wait until dinner.'

The look that emanates from my dearly beloved's eyes would make a gorgon proud.

That'll be a no, then.

CARRY ON UP THE DANUBE

We've been told that a river cruise is very relaxing, so we're trying one up the Danube—to coin a phrase.

Anyway, after a long journey to Budapest, I can't wait for my head to hit the pillow. It's three o'clock in the morning when I discover that our comfy cabin is masquerading as a total death trap.

I get up to use the facilities and tiptoe to the toilet in the dark so as not to wake DB, who, unsurprisingly, is snoring loud enough to wake most of the citizens of Budapest. It's then that I forget about the trip hazard that seems to feature in every ship's cabin: the 6-inch sill between the bedroom and bathroom. My toe catches the top of the sill, and I'm unceremoniously catapulted into the bathroom. My foot slips on the bathmat and, before I know it, like Oliver Reed on a bender, I've done a purler headfirst into the shower.

Don't worry, I think, DB will have heard that and come and rescue me. But not a bit of it. DB snores on. I pick myself up and, slightly shaken, tiptoe back to bed.

But the fun isn't over yet. The cramped, dark cabin means the arm of a lurking chair manages to damn near kneecap me.

Feeling that I'd gone ten rounds with Giant Haystacks, it takes some time before I feel sleepy again.

DB wakes up.

'Watch the step,' I murmur.

Does he take a leaf out of my book and creep about quietly? No, not at all! ZAP! On goes DB's 'handy' torch—the kind that's tiny in size but has a beam so bright that it could top any would-be Gestapo agent's Christmas list. That does it; I'm instantly wide awake.

DB disappears into the bathroom, and the room is blissfully quiet and dark again.

I'm just drifting pleasantly back to sleep once more when a deafening noise, like a herd of flatulent hippos, snaps me awake again. DB has flushed the toilet, which works on the same deafening suction principle as the ones on an aeroplane—but with knobs on. Let's just say there's more chance of surviving an encounter with a Black Hole than this toilet.

DB weaves his way back to bed, with his mega-powerful torch beam blinding me anew with every stride. A lighthouse keeper would feel instantly at home here, I muse.

He climbs into bed and, at last, all is peaceful. I turn over and cough quietly once, then twice.

'Are you going to cough all night?' DB asks grumpily. 'That's going to be really irritating!'

***

At the end of this morning's trip, we're told we have some free time before the boat sets sail again.

'Just enough time to track down some nail varnish,' I say.

DB, being a fella, doesn't get it—one bit.

'Nail varnish?' he queries.

'You do know we're in the depths of the Wachau Valley; it's not exactly renowned for its branches of Boots!'

I ignore him.

'Look!' I say, 'There's a little supermarket. I might get some there!'

DB looks at me with despair in his eyes, but we go in and look around. DB's right. Not a drop of nail varnish to be seen.

Then I spot a lady who's obviously a local.

'Do you speak English?' I ask.

'Nein,' she replies.

That's a bummer, I think, but undaunted, carry on.

'Nail varnish?' I ask.

She looks at me blankly.

'I'm looking....' I mime, shading my eyes with one hand and doing an exaggerated look right and then an exaggerated look left like an inept sailor's hornpipe.

No response. I try again.

'Looking....' I say slowly and repeat the mime.

'Oh good, is it charades?' quips DB.

I sigh deeply. Idiot.

'For NAIL,' I say loudly, 'VARNISH.'

'I've got it! It's B&Q!' says DB. 'Nails; varnish—got to be B&Q.'

'We're not playing charades!' I growl.

I glance at my watch and realise that with all the shenanigans, we're due back on board in a few minutes.

'Come on! We've got to go!' I say to DB, who mutters something about it not being his stupid idea to look for nail varnish in the back of beyond.

As we hot-foot it back to the boat, the heavens open. We huddle together under my very small umbrella and start a semi-jog. All I can say is jogging in tandem while sharing a brolly requires the same amount of skill as an Olympic sport.

We bump into each other like a pair of drunks in a three-legged race, while the umbrella spokes do their best to poke out the eye of the person not carrying it. Bad luck, DB.

Amid squawks of outrage from DB and inane giggling from me, we make it back to the boat just as two swarthy crew members are hovering worryingly around the gangplank.

It's only then we realise that we just abandoned the lady in the supermarket without even an 'auf wiedersehen.'

'Dummkopfs!' she's probably thinking.

***

We're visiting the beautiful town of Passau today. Its cathedral houses the world's largest church organ, so a lunchtime concert is a must.

The cathedral is vast, holding 1200 people, and today, it's filled to the rafters. It's not long before the organist takes her place. She is a Domkapellmeisterin, whatever that is, but it's a safe bet if she's been let loose on the world's biggest organ; it means she's probably past the 'Chopsticks' stage. She starts her recital, and organ music fills this enormous cathedral, blasting out the glorious music of Bach. 1200 heads lift upwards, relishing the wonderful amalgam of music and stunning architecture.

Correction.

1199 heads lift upwards—because DB, chin on chest, is having a dose!

The organist is letting rip, the whole cathedral reverberating with the sound. Even the inhabitants of the crypt are stuffing their fingers in their ears, but this is DB… DB, who could manage forty winks in the midst of a nuclear holocaust.

I fix him with a stare which says, dare snore, and a re-run of 'Murder in the Cathedral' could be on the cards. But DB slumbers peacefully on. That is until the organist reaches a particularly thunderous bit where she pulls out all the stops—literally. DB wakes with a start, 'Whassat?' he says. I poke him fiercely in the ribs while a dozen angry faces whirl around to find out which eejit in the fifth row would dare disturb the esteemed Domkapellmeisterin.

The concert finishes, and we escape sharpish before DB is lynched by a mob of angry Bavarians.

It's been a sweltering day, so later that evening, before settling down for the night, I turn up the air conditioning in the cabin.

'What are you doing?' asks DB with horror.

'It's so hot I've turned up the air conditioning,' I say.

'You can't do that!' DB says, outraged. 'I'll never get to sleep!'

CLUELESS TECHNOLOGY

It was all going so well. We'd had a lovely time in Scotland, meeting old friends and enjoying some trips down memory lane. DB had behaved himself all week and had not done anything silly at all. Then….

We arrive at our stopover hotel on our journey home, unload the car, and check-in. DB conveniently remembers his newspaper, which is in the boot, so he goes back to the car while I stagger into the lift with two suitcases, a rucksack, my handbag, a litre bottle of water, and the lunch bag. I look like a cross between an Olympic weightlifter and an out-of-work Sherpa.

I'm gasping my last, spread-eagled on the bed, when DB returns in a right two-and-eight saying the car boot won't lock!

'But it was locked this morning when we went to pack the car,' I remind him.

'Well, it won't lock now! I've been trying to lock it for the past ten minutes, and every time I check if it's locked, it opens again.'

'Brilliant,' I say with an air of weary inevitability. I should have known that a hassle-free trip was a pipe dream.

'Now, what do we do?' I ask.

'Well, we can't leave it open overnight, and we're miles from a garage, so we'll have to sleep in the car.'

'Er, wait a minute,' I say. What's with the Royal 'we?' It's your car, YOU sleep in it overnight!'

DB goes selectively deaf and begins poring over the manual in the hope it might reveal some magic solution.

Now, the car, which we've only had for a few months, has every gadget and gizmo known to man, so making sense of the manual needs a PhD in Advanced Electronics. Unfortunately, the nearest DB has got—is a Boy Scout badge in model aircraft, so it's safe to say he's none the wiser.

There's much frantic flicking through pages and heaving of sighs when he suddenly throws down the manual and declares,

'This is stupid! How are you supposed to understand all this gobbledygook!'

'It's only gobbledygook to you, dear,' I say. 'Probably child's play to anyone with a modicum of technological nous.' He gives me his best thunderous look.

'Look,' I suggest, 'ring a VW garage and ask them if they can suggest something.'

It's obvious he's not revelling in the prospect of being told what to do by a quote, 'snotty-nosed youngster just out of short trousers', but eventually swallows his pride and rings.

I listen in to the call, keeping everything crossed that a solution is found, as I'm not relishing the prospect of spending the night in my PJs in a draughty car.

After explaining the problem, the voice at the other end says. 'When you keep trying the boot, and it's unlocked, are your keys in your hand?'

DB looks at me and raises his eyes to the heavens as if to say, 'Where else would they be? Outer Mongolia!'

'You see, sir,' the mechanic continues slowly, apparently convinced that DB is a spanner short of a socket set. 'The car senses when the key is in range and automatically opens the boot for you.'

There is a long silence, then….

'Really?' says DB, lost for any other response.

'Yes, sir, it's called keyless technology.'

More like 'clueless technology' where DB's concerned, is my immediate thought but say nothing.

'Never knew that. How marvellous,' DB continues to babble. 'Thank you.'

He puts down the phone and splutters, outraged, 'Never heard anything so ridiculous. How are you supposed to know that! Blooming stupid technology!'

I say nothing…. just quietly rejoice that I'll be sleeping in a nice comfy bed and not the back seat of the car!

COMPRENEZ-VOUS?

You'd assume if you were French and saw someone frantically flicking through a dog-eared French phrase book saying, 'Qu'est-ce que c'est?' in a dodgy franglais accent, that you'd take the hint and speak 'lentement' and not at the rate of a rapid-fire machine gun!

Mais non! Here in France, whenever I've asked a simple question, I've had an answer that involves a volley of complicated vocabulary that even Emanuel Macron would find difficult! So, what chance has a Glaswegian? A Glaswegian, by the way, who is also a bit Mutt and Jeff. None.

Therefore, when I discover that the owners of the Honfleur hotel where we're staying are also Glaswegian, I'm 'sur la lune!' as they say here. No more scratching my head and trying to translate at warp speed. But wrong! These two are like the Crankies on crack—both speak, usually simultaneously, with impenetrable Glaswegian accents. Now, you'd think that would be no problem for me, but these two would make Rab C Nesbitt sound like Prince Charles. When I ask where the Satie exhibition is, it goes something like this.

'Oh aye, no' far.'

'It's aboot a huner' metres frae the quay.'

'Naw, mair 'an 'at!'

'Naw, it's no!'

'Ach, awa and bile yir heid, ye stumer.'

(Ok, I might have made that last bit up!)

'What did they say?' asks DB later, who is equally bemused whether he's listening to French or Glaswegian.

'Er, not sure,' I reply.

'Not sure? That was your mother tongue!' DB says disappointedly.

'Yes, well, do you understand strong cockney?' I argue.

'Yep, no trouble. Gor blimey, guvnor/Dahn the old Bull and Bush/Luv a duck!' he says, sounding like Dick van Dyke on a bad day.

There is a pause while DB racks his brains for another handy Cockney phrase or saying.

'Apples and pears, er....'

'My point exactly!'

Anyway, I've taken a stab in the dark at what they've said, so it's anybody's guess whether we'll find the museum or not. But as us Scots say, 'We'll gie it a go!'

DB, THE VIKING

So, we're on a cruise to the Norwegian Fjords, me and my not so able-bodied seaman, DB—aka my Dearly Beloved.

Life on board ship certainly provides interesting experiences—especially when you're new to the world of cruising. When you're first on board, you have to attend a safety briefing at your designated muster point. In the cabin, we listened to the captain's instructions: 'On the abandon ship signal, bring your life jacket, warm clothing, a head covering, and any medicines you normally take.'

The practice signal sounds, and I grab my life jacket. DB, always a stickler for the rules, has donned a fleece and a hat and is carrying a bag of medicines that would sink most respectable battleships.

'What're you doing?' I ask.

'Doing what the captain said,' he replies.

'But this is just a practice,' I say. 'You just need the lifejacket, not half your wardrobe!'

'Yes, but if you were to end up in the North Sea, it'd be freezing; you'd be glad of a jacket then.'

'Yes, but we're not going to end up in the sea, are we? IT'S A PRACTICE!'

But did DB listen? No. He sets off trussed up to the eyeballs like an Arctic explorer.

Now, we're supposed to muster in one of the large restaurants, but because of numbers, we spill over into a small bar area. A very warm and cramped bar area. It doesn't take long before DB is feeling overheated. Beads of perspiration begin to drip down his face which is getting redder and redder by the minute. And is anyone else there in a similar get-up? No, of course not. Every other sane person is in a T-shirt and shorts, looking on in bewildered amusement. DB's just about to peel off a layer when the crew tell us to don our life jackets.

'Heck,' I think. 'Another layer for him to contend with!'

I look over to see DB grappling to get into his life jacket. The hat he's been wearing has been knocked over his eyes; because he needed two hands to tie the lifejacket, he's clamped the enormous bag of medicine between his legs, and his arms are stuck out sideways due to the bulk of the lifejacket plus his thick jacket. If you can imagine a puce-faced, knock-kneed Wurzel Gummidge, that's a pretty accurate picture! And he's my husband! Aaaargh!

Thankfully, the drill is soon over, and we return to the cabin. DB needs a lie down after the trauma of it all, and I just pray that we never have to abandon ship because I can't stand going through all that palaver again!

***

This evening someone recommends the Crow's Nest bar for a drink after dinner as it has a magnificent panoramic window with a great view. Now, as the name suggests, it's somewhere at the top of the ship, but where exactly? We use the lift to the top floor, but no joy; there's not a crow in sight, let alone a nest. Stumped, we go on deck and look up and see a place with a massive glass window which looks forward or 'for'ard', as us sea dogs say.

'That must be it,' I say.

'Are you sure?' DB queries, as ever, suspicious of any of my directions.

'Look, it's right at the top of the ship and it's got a huge window. That's got to be it.'

We find some stairs and spot a barrier which says 'no admittance' but, as it's been pushed back flush with the wall, we assume it's ok to go up.

We're now on the very top deck, and it's blowing a hoolie.

'Hurry up and get inside,' yells DB. 'This wind's giving me gyp.'

'Nothing new there,' I think, but say nowt.

We head over to where there's a door to get out of the wind.

As we get closer, I can see some twinkling red and green lights through the dark glass.

'Oh, look, that's pretty,' I say to DB.

DB stops dead in his tracks.

'What's wrong?'

'Why are all the people in there dressed in uniform?'

'Are they?' I reply, peering through the gloom.

'For Pete's sake, Fiona. That's not the Crow's Nest; that's the flaming bridge! Run before we're arrested.'

Now, have you ever tried running against a gale-force wind? Let me tell you, it's the stuff of nightmares. Everything happens in slow motion. Your legs are going like the clappers, but you're not getting anywhere. Eventually, we get back inside, totally windswept. The sophisticated image I was aiming for has gone for a burton. My hair looks like Marge Simpson on a bad day, and even the little bit that DB's got left looks like he's had his fingers in an electrical socket.

Defeated, we go back to our cabin. Perhaps we'll try another bar tomorrow night.

***

The lifts on the ship seem to have a mind of their own. They might stop at your floor, or they might go sailing past. It's true to say they can be a bit 'up and down', not very 'elevating', hardly 'uplifting'. Ok, enough of the duff lift jokes.

There are three sets on every floor. One in the middle of a very wide landing and one at either side. The trick is to second-guess which one is going to arrive first.

DB and I have devised a system where we push all the buttons on all the lifts and then adopt a half-crouched position - two decrepit Mo Farrahs at the start line - ready to make a mad dash for whichever one comes first. However, the system is not foolproof. The lift you opt for can often be already full, while the one you've spurned sails past empty.

Today is particularly frustrating. We've damn near worn a trough in the carpet by scampering between lifts like a pair of deranged hamsters.

At last, one arrives, but as usual, I'm loitering at the wrong end of the hallway, much to DB's annoyance.

'Hurry up—we're going to miss this one too,' he grumbles and sticks one of his enormous size 11s in the door to stop it closing before I get there.

I quickly jump in, but now the lift seems totally narked off by the size 11 interference because the doors start to open and close willy-nilly. Open, close, open, close.

'Ooh, that's not good!' I say warily. 'Let's get out.'

Unfortunately, we both make for the closing doors at the same time, jamming ourselves shoulder to shoulder between them like a second-rate comedy duo. We step back quickly, but as far as the lift is concerned, insult has been added to injury, and its doors go completely loopy.

'You've scrambled its brains, now,' says DB ignoring the fact it was one of his great clodhoppers who started it all.

After some more frantic pressing of buttons, the doors stay closed, and we go down.

All is well….

until it whizzes past the floor we want.

DB presses a few more buttons.

It goes up….

and whizzes past the floor we want.

DB is apoplectic. 'Right!' he yells at the wayward lift. 'You've got one more chance, or we're taking the stairs.'

Fearing that any more indiscriminate pushing of buttons might launch us up through the sky deck and into the sea, I persuade him to admit defeat and take the stairs.

Later in the day, we pass the same stroppy lift, now proudly exhibiting a large OUT OF ORDER sign.

'What a nuisance!' grumbles a fellow passenger. 'It was working perfectly earlier today.'

'Really?' we say sympathetically and scarper sharpish.

We dock the following day back in Southampton. As we totter down the gangplank with our luggage, we spot a van with the words OTIS LIFTS emblazoned on the side.

'Keep your head down!' DB cautions, 'and say nothing!'

HASTA LA VISTA!

We Bundells, totally fed up with the cold air of the UK, decide to swap it for the hot air of Gran Canaria. But there's trouble before we even start!

We arrive at the reception of the airport parking site, hand over the car keys to the parking attendant, and get on the shuttle bus to wait for our transfer to the terminal. All is well, until I spot our car drive past the bus on its way to wherever they park cars on a long-term basis.

'Oh, look,' I say to DB, 'there's our car.' We look out of the bus window and watch it sail past when suddenly DB turns deathly pale.

'No!' he shouts. 'My bag's still on the back seat!'

That wouldn't be just any old bag; that would be the bag which contains his wallet, phone, and passport, and now it is winging its way to Lord knows where for a week.

Before I can say 'Hasta la vista,' DB has leapt off the bus and sets off in hot pursuit, waving his arms wildly and screaming 'Stop!' at the top of his voice.

Blissfully unaware of the frenzy behind him, the car park attendant blithely drives on. Dodgy ankles and dicky ticker notwithstanding, DB tries to do his Superman 'faster than a speeding bullet' impersonation, but he is never going to outrun a fast-moving car.

I am just debating whether to kill him in full view of a bus load of people or wait until we are alone, when the car suddenly screeches to a halt and then reverses at speed back the way it came. Someone in reception has obviously seen DB's hysterics and radioed the driver that the imminent demise of an OAP is on the cards, so get back to reception ASAP.

Reunited at last with his man bag, DB re-boards the bus panting, puffing, and more than a little crimson in the complexion. The waiting passengers, wondering if DB is about to gasp his last, suddenly change from being mutinous to drawing lots for who is going to give this old geezer the kiss of life.

I contemplate saving them the bother and finishing him off completely but think better of it and we set off for the terminal.

All this before we've even left the country!

***

Feeling the need for some relaxation after the nightmare of the previous day, we resolve to spend our time resting around the pool. DB decides a swim is in order and gets into the pool, sucking in everything that can be sucked in, and begins a gentle breaststroke through the water.

A young Adonis, all golden tan and rippling six-pack, dives in the other side. He backstrokes smoothly down the length of the pool with long, powerful strokes. DB watches with envy. Having been married to him for 40-odd years (emphasis on the odd), I know exactly what he's thinking.

'I was once a great swimmer like that.'

The cogs whirr...

'I'll show that young whipper snapper a thing or two,' he thinks.

DB flips over and swims on his back, strokes not quite so long and powerful these days, but I can tell he's thinking, 'Not bad for an old codger.'

He's just picked up a decent speed when there's an audible *CLUNK!* DB misjudges the length of the pool and crashes headfirst into the side.

A few watching sunbathers wince, others don't know whether to laugh or administer first aid.

'All right, darling?' I ask blithely.

Slightly dazed, DB staggers out of the pool, trying to look as if nearly braining himself was all part of the plan.

Meanwhile, the young Adonis continues to slice through the water, oblivious to DB's embarrassing moment.

What is it that saying about pride coming before a fall? Or should that be swim?

***

Having had a touch of Delhi belly, I decide to starve myself for most of the day.

By dinner time, I am FAMISHED! I opt for tomato soup with cream and basil. The waiter arrives with the soup...which is quite clearly carrot and lentil.

'Excuse me,' I say politely. 'This isn't tomato soup.'

The waiter looks at it.

'Si, tomato soup," he nods vigorously.

'No, I ordered tomato soup with cream and basil.' I point to it on the menu.

'Si, tomato soup,' he nods again.

Realising he was definitely a product of the Basil Fawlty school of waiters, I resort to pidgin English. 'This no right soup. This wrong soup.'

'Ah, wrong soup!' he says. 'I bring different soup!'

He returns with more soup.... consommé this time. No cream, no basil, and not a tomato in sight.

I take a deep breath.

'This-no-to-ma-to sooop,' I over enunciate.

'Si, tomato soup,' he nods even more vigorously.

I give up and go straight for the main course. Guinea fowl with plum sauce sounds nice.

Now, at this point, I should explain that our waiter is called Vasili. Vasili is from Ukraine, working in a German hotel in a Spanish resort and trying to speak English, so you'd think I would have learned my lesson by now, and eschew any further conversation, but no. Wary that the sauce may be a bit rich for my dicky tummy, I foolishly ask, 'Could I have the sauce on the side?'

'Que?' replies Vasili.

'The sauce. On the side?' I make a circle with my thumb and forefinger to demonstrate a small pot.

'Que?' replies Vasili. (Or should that be Manuel.)

'THE - PLUM - SAUCE,' I say very slowly and very loudly. 'NO-ON-PLATE. IN POT....' and I mime again what to me is quite clearly a small pot.

'Ah, si!' says Vasili as understanding finally dawns. 'You want a pot on the side!'

'Si, por favor, gracias!' I say, mustering the only three Spanish phrases in my lexicon.

A few minutes later a small leg of guinea fowl arrives. Nothing else on the plate. Then, with a proud flourish, Vasili produces... a small glass of neat port! Clearly, the difference between 'pot' and 'port' has been lost in translation.

He smiles triumphantly but then, seeing the thunderous look on my face, quickly legs it to the far side of the restaurant, probably to hand in his notice.

The plain guinea fowl is looking a tad dry, I have to say, so nothing ventured...I tentatively pour a little of the port onto my meat. Now, I don't know if you've ever tried hot guinea fowl swimming in a pool of cold port, but it's safe to say it won't be on the menu at The Ivy any time soon! I eat a few mouthfuls and throw in the towel.

As you can imagine, this fiasco has taken some time to play out.

DB, meanwhile, has worked his way through tuna tartare, prawn and cream flan, herb-crusted salmon, assorted ice creams, and cheese and biscuits.

I was just about to get my chops around a decent pud when he says, 'Phew! I've eaten too much. Do you really need that pudding? I need to go and loosen my trousers!'

Suffice it to say, my paltry knowledge of Spanish has just been extended to 'Where is the nearest divorce court!'

***

We are feeling a little out of place in this German-owned hotel, so today, I am trying to persuade DB to join the aqua aerobics session in the pool. For someone who's keen on fitness, he seems strangely reluctant. I don't know why, for Helga, the German instructor, is tall, tanned and blonde. Mind you, she's also built like a brick outhouse! She barks out her commands, has a steely eye that brooks no argument and demands that her acolytes move in perfect unison. Falter at any point, and she goes into full Gruppenfuhrer mode. DB decides to give it a miss.

So, we're lying on the only sun beds available after the usual early morning German blitzkrieg. These sunbeds—not surprisingly—are the ones which are about two miles from the pool and in the impenetrable shade! Not that this worries DB, who, having been a bit of a 'ging-er ' in his youth, burns to a crisp if he even looks at a bottle of Amber Solaire, while I, in contrast, have been fighting off frostbite for most of the morning.

I'm lying there shivering when suddenly there are shouts of 'Dummkopf' and 'Gott in Himmel' as all-out warfare is declared between two rival German couples over sun bed possession. Germanic insults fly through the air, and soon, the rest of their fellow sun worshippers are divided into two opposing factions.

DB and I look surreptitiously at each other and make a decision that feigned nonchalance is the best course of action. DB does some silent whistling—always a sign he's feeling uncomfortable—and I quickly bury my head in a book—a little island of British calm in the midst of Armageddon!

Eventually, after there's been a good deal of angry shunting of sun loungers back and forth, a middle ground is reached, and a fragile peace is declared. Relieved, we slink away before more German ire is provoked when they realise we're not fellow countrymen but the *conquering British*. Not sure what would be worse: some Teutonic retribution—or an aqua aerobics session with Helga!

***

So, it's our last night in Gran Canaria, and excitement is in the air. The hotel has informed everyone that a drone will be flying overhead, taking pictures for a promotional video.

The place is a hotbed of meticulous German preparation. Sunbeds are lined up in uniform ranks, parasols are collapsed and precisely spaced, and the staff are spitting and polishing all over the place.

Each room has had a letter outlining how we guests can play our part: vacate the pool area by the stated time; don't hang towels, etc, on the balconies; and stay off the balconies while the drone is overhead.

DB, never one to read instructions for anything (as a number of our slightly wonky pieces of IKEA furniture will testify), doesn't see the bit about staying off the balcony. Allegedly.

He is just getting dressed after a shower when he hears the sound of the drone overhead and, desperate not to miss this photographic coup, rushes out there with his camera. Now, being on the balcony is a problem in itself, but to compound the felony... he just happens to be in his underpants. Not the swish David Beckham type, you understand, but ones which, shall we say, have seen better days!

'What are you doing!' I shout. 'You're not supposed to be out there!'

I picture the manager monitoring the drone pictures on a screen somewhere, puce in the face and screaming, 'Nein, Nein!' as DB wrecks the carefully stage-managed view of his hotel.

'Who iz ze Dummkopf in zimmer 352? He iz ruining every zing! Mein Gott, he iz in his underpants! Und Gott in Himmel, they have seen better days! Zis iz ein disaster!'

Then, watching as a disembodied female arm appears, and pulls the Dummkopf off the balcony by the back of said underpants.

Yep, that probably made his day.

Anyway, if at any time you are doing a recce on hotels in Gran Canaria and you come across a promotional video with a bloke on a balcony sporting a not-too-snazzy line in underwear, that'll be DB!

So, despite a gippy tummy, non-compliant waiters, German warfare, and an unexpected feature in a Trip Advisor video, we've had a great holiday. So, until next time—'Adios' or should that be 'Auf Weidersehen!'

I AM A DALEK!

Problems at airports country-wide have been well documented in the news recently, so we don't hold out much hope for a smooth journey when we set off for another jaunt tomorrow. Little do we know that our problems will begin long before that!

We are due to set off at the unearthly hour of 3 a.m. In a desperate attempt to get some sleep before the journey, I'm in my nightie almost before 'Countdown' starts. My Dearly Beloved just guffaws at my suggestion for an early night, which, in another era, might have put a major glint in his eye, but that's another story!

Anyway, I toss and turn for hours to no avail. I'm just drifting off when DB thunders in. The door bursts open; I'm blinded by the bedside light and bounced off the mattress as he does his usual backdrop into bed. It takes nanoseconds before the snoring starts, while I lie awake counting enough sheep to populate a Yorkshire hill farm!

At last, the alarm rings, and we set off for Gatwick. We're taking my car with no sat nav, so we use Google maps on my phone to find the airport car park. No problem, you'd think. Google Maps—very reliable. All is hunky dory until we reach a diversion due to road works. We can actually see the airport, but Mr Google decides that the best route is to drive two miles down a dual carriageway in the opposite direction! Being good, law-abiding citizens, we follow instructions, only to be told at the end of the road to do a U-turn and drive for two miles back the way we've just come! This happens twice more, so we've now driven 12 miles in circles! The time for check-in is getting uncomfortably close, so we go rogue and head towards the airport willy-nilly. In the meantime, I'm trying to fathom what's wrong with my phone. I load Google Maps again but now it's repeatedly giving directions on how to *walk* to the car park! I take a leaf out of DB's book and begin screaming at an inanimate object.

'I don't want to walk to the stupid car park, you half-wit. I'm in a car!'

'Walk half a mile and take a right turn,' it intones back sweetly.

'Why does it keep telling us to walk?' says DB. 'What's wrong with it?'

'How should I know! Stop asking stupid questions!' I scream.

DB sees that I'm near to the end of my one remaining wit and says meekly, 'It's just that I've been driving around this same roundabout for quite a while now!'

I look at my watch and see that check-in is even closer. In desperation, we plump for a random turning and finally, with a huge sigh of relief, spy the long-term car park in the distance and head towards it. Despite a dead end and a risky, and undoubtedly illegal, cut through via a service road, we finally arrive at the car park.

We approach the car park barrier, which opens automatically but doesn't issue us a ticket. We assume that no ticket means we can park in any available spot, so we choose the first car park we come to, which, for some unknown reason, is signposted, 'Robotised Parking'.

'What the heck does that mean?' I query.

'Look, we're late, and it's a car park,' says DB. 'I don't care if Robocop himself parks the car, as long as we get to the terminal before winter sets in!'

We pile out of the car and head for the bus stop.

'Wait!' I yell as I notice that the interior car light, which I'd switched on to see my phone better, is still on. DB screeches to a halt, scrabbles for the car key, and I hotfoot it back to the car. I flick a switch, slam the door, and begin wheeling my case back towards DB.

'You haven't switched it off!' shouts DB, miming to turn back.

'Yes, I have!'

'No, you haven't! It's still on.'

'No, it isn't.'

'Yes, it is!'

'No, it isn....' I look over my shoulder... 'Yes, it is!'

I return to the car and try a different switch. Thus begins the never-ending loop of frantic light switch flicking interspersed by bad-tempered slamming of the car door to check if the light is off.

'What ARE you doing?! Let me do it!' DB growls.

At last, he finds the right combination of rocker switch and light switch, and thankfully, the car interior is plunged into darkness.

We get to the bus stop to wait for an airport bus and wait….and wait…

We've wasted so much time

a) driving around in circles

b) being bamboozled by the mysteries of electric circuitry that a non-existent bus is the final straw. We push the help button and ask if a bus is due. A voice replies. Or at least we think it's a voice. The sound quality is so bad we can't decipher a word.

'Pardon?' DB shouts but the disembodied voice has gone. DB pushes the button again. The voice returns, and we repeat the question. 'You need to azrgh chklou hjit,' it replies and disappears again.

'This is ridiculous!' DB splutters, 'This is this robotised thing, isn't it!? I'm speaking to a flaming Dalek!' It's now his turn to fume. He stabs the button for a third time.

'Now, look here,' he declaims, 'This is beyond a joke. We've got a plane to catch, and there's no bus. Can someone give us an answer that we can understand?'

At last, another voice answers—still with definite overtones of Bill and Ben—but decipherable.

'You are in the wrong car park. You need to go to Car Park B.'

We look around us and see a huge letter B about 300 metres away, where an airport bus is waiting.

'Get in the car!' DB yells and then adds, 'And DON'T touch the light switches!'

I do as I'm told, and we set off like Mutley and Dastardly cornering on two wheels accompanied by some serious cutting up of a few brassed-off drivers.

We fling the car into a space and then race to the waiting bus.

At the terminal, completely wrung out by the whole ordeal of catching the plane on time, we see that the flight has been delayed by two hours! Marvellous.

I NO SPEAKA DA LINGO

DB and I have just landed at our favourite place, Gran Canaria, to grab some winter sunshine. Surprisingly, there has been none of the drama of previous holiday mishaps— no unexpected detours, missing boarding passes, or even a smidgen of banana gate. (see Viva Espana!). In fact, the journey to the airport, check-in, security, etc., all go without a hitch.

We should have known better....

The airport bus delivers us to the hotel and the luggage is unloaded and taken into reception.

'You must have a welcome drink, senor,' says the receptionist, 'We will take the luggage to your room.'

'Great,' says DB, who is keen to get into the holiday spirit ASAP.

We go off to the bar, enjoy a leisurely drink, and then go up to the room to unpack.

I'm powdering my nose when I hear some ripe language emanating from the bedroom.

'I don't believe it! This is not my sodding suitcase!' yells DB.

I rush out of the loo to see an identical case to DB's lying on the bed. Well, almost identical. It's black; it's rectangular, but there the similarity ends.

Now, this is a problem—not just about DB being lumbered with someone else's smalls for the week—but because potentially, not to put too fine a point on it, it's a matter of life and death. In DB's suitcase is a raft of heart tablets which literally keep him tickety-boo, with the emphasis on 'TICK-ety.'

DB phones reception in a panic to tell them that they must have delivered his luggage to the wrong room, but after contacting everyone in the hotel who arrived on the same airport bus, the case is still AWOL.

It's safe to say that DB's holiday joie de vivre has well and truly vanished, so it's probably not a good time to mention that it's a pity my duty-free perfume, which was in the case, has also gone missing.

'Oh dear,' DB utters without a modicum of sympathy. 'Such a shame you'll not smell nice, but frankly, I'm not sure anyone will notice a) when I've been wearing the same pair of boxers for a week or b) when I'm suffering cardiac arrest!'

Fair point.

I'm just about to brush up on my CPR when the phone rings.

'This is Mrs Bundell? No?' says a Spanish voice at the other end.

'Yes,' I say.

'You have a missing case? No?'

'Yes,' I say.

'It iz at ze wrong hotel,' the voice says. 'I will breeng it to you now. No?'

'Yes, yes, please.'

I relay the good news to DB and a hasty exchange of identical suitcases, which wouldn't look amiss in a Bond movie, soon takes place in reception. DB is delighted to be reunited with his underwear, emergency services on the island can stand down and, best of all, I will be smelling fragrant for the entire week.

***

'How about a walk today?' suggests DB. 'I've worked out a route that will take us to a lovely nature reserve.'

I look at the map which DB's holding and wonder if he's completely lost his marbles. It's one of those freebies which looks like it's been drawn by a blindfolded toddler gone rampant with a box of cheap crayons. There's a patch of blue—sea; a patch of yellow—sand; some random white lines—roads; and a green area with what looks like a few sprigs of broccoli—trees. DB's pointing at the broccoli.

'Seriously?' I query, 'and that's the map we're using?'

'One map is as good as another when you've been a Boy Scout,' DB says confidently.

Not sure Baden Powell would see it that way I think, but not wanting to dampen DB's enthusiasm, we set off.

It all starts rather promisingly with a walk by the impressive sand dunes, but then, following the trusty map, we turn inland. Sea and sand are replaced by a desolated urban wasteland.

DB scratches his head turning the map this way and that.

'Problem?' I say suspiciously.

'No, no,' says DB, never one to admit defeat. 'It's just we should be here!' he insists, his finger prodding a patch of broccoli.

'Just exactly how long was your stint in the Boy Scouts?' I question, 'cos your map reading skills are not worth a woggle!'

DB ignores me.

Forty-five minutes later, things haven't improved. I've been treated to the picturesque sights of a dual carriageway, an abandoned car park, a building site, and, oh yes, how could I forget the highlight of the trip—a cement mixer!

I spot a sign that says 'Meloneras'—where this fiasco started. 'Right! That's it!' I declare in my best no-nonsense voice. 'Mission abandoned as far as I'm concerned. Stuff the map, I'm off!' And so, I dump the intrepid Bear Grylls and head off for the comforts of the hotel.

***

Our holiday in Gran Canaria has been beautiful. The weather is wonderful, the hotel stunning, and we've thoroughly enjoyed relaxing in this lovely place... until the last day.

As it's another beautiful morning, I decide to do a power walk.

I'm enjoying the peace and tranquillity when I decide to liven things up by falling at full pelt, chin first, flat on my face onto a concrete pavement. DB, back at the hotel, is blissfully unaware that I'm lying in a heap bleeding so profusely I could be an extra in a particularly grisly episode of CSI.

Along with bucketfuls of blood, both wrists are sprained, and my knees seem well and truly knackered.

I eventually manage to get hold of my phone, ring DB and groan that I need help.

Just as he arrives, a very kind taxi driver, worrying that my impression of a murder victim is giving this rather upmarket area a bad name, scoops me up and drives us to the nearest hospital.

Then, the fun begins.

I don't speaka da lingo, and the doctor has only a smattering of English.

I mime walking and then gesture 'falling over' with my hands. However, I'm so shaken up that my walk turns into a stagger, which, combined with trembling hands, just makes me look like a serious drunk with a bad case of the DTs.

The doctor points to my chin, which is split wide open and still gushing blood, and says comfortingly, 'Chin, very bad! Need many stitchings—muchos pain.' Then he adds more encouragingly, 'Head not bad as much.'

Oh, that's good, I think, but not for long as he carries on, 'Still need stitchings—still muchos pain.'

With these cheery words, he brandishes a syringe with sadistic glee and begins injecting anaesthetic into every few millimetres of my face. I can tell you; those Spaniards don't lie!

In a bid to take my mind off the muchos pain, I quip that if this is what Botox is like, I'll give it a miss, but it gets lost in translation. So does my suggestion when he's stitching my chin that, for aesthetic reasons, he takes in a few spare inches of the old turkey neck.

Next thing I know, I'm having a CT scan, an ECG, and, quite frankly, the most unpleasant of the lot, a COVID test done with so much Spanish gusto that the swab almost comes out the top of my head!

Unable to think up any more torture, he bids me farewell with the order, 'You no washing for seven days till stitchings come out.'

In my foggy state of mind, I initially think, 'Blimey, I'll be humming by then.' But then realise he probably means my hair…, doesn't he?

At last, we get back to the hotel, DB in a state of shock with it all and me looking like a patched-up Saturday night drunk!

By the evening, when I literally stagger down to dinner, aka any unappetising mush that can be sucked up through a straw, I'm developing a very attractive shiner plus a schnozzle the size of Cyrano de Bergerac's.

A fellow Glaswegian, seeing the huge white dressings covering half my face, asks after my welfare, then with typical Glaswegian humour adds, 'Mind you, yir tan's gonnae be interesting!'

I'd have laughed if it wasn't for the stitchings and the muchos pain!

OH, I DO LIKE TO BE BESIDE THE SEASIDE

We're here in the beautiful Gower in Wales for the August Bank Holiday, which, surprisingly for an English Bank Holiday, has turned out to be positively tropical!

Good, you might think, just what you want on holiday. Not necessarily. Not when you've packed for wet Welsh hiking.

DB, who always thinks that anywhere north of Watford Gap is akin to the Arctic Circle, has brought along a nice line in padded gilets and double cable knits, and I'm not much better with long trousers, a couple of sweatshirts and a pair of hiking boots.

We've unpacked the car, and I'm making a welcome cuppa when, out of the blue, DB suddenly says, 'Let's have a walk along the beach.' I wonder what the rush is, then look down from our balcony to see an array of particularly comely sun worshippers, all blonde highlights and no cellulite, and suddenly, it becomes clear!

'And what particular item of winter clothing have we brought that's going to allow us to walk along a beach of half-naked sunbathers without looking so out of place that we'll be locked up in the nearest asylum, pronto?' I ask. 'Walking boots? A fleece? Waterproof jacket?'

'Come on, nobody's going to take any notice. It's a shame to waste the sun.'

So off we go, like Ernest Shackleton and his missus, DB sweltering in a thick shirt and jeans while my token effort of rolling my trousers up to my knees makes me a dead ringer for one of those old dears that you see on cheap seaside postcards.

Having survived the muffled titters (sorry, still in cheap seaside postcard mode) of our fellow beachgoers, plus narrowly escaping heatstroke, sunstroke, not to mention a proper stroke in those blistering temperatures, we decide that a trip into town for something cooler is a necessity.

We set off with a skip in our step, looking forward to negating our reputation amongst the locals of the overdressed vagrant couple with the faces of two well-boiled lobsters. Sadly, the 'skip' soon becomes a plod as we realise that Bank Holiday in small-town Wales means the only shops open are Tesco Express and the local branch of Specsavers, neither renowned for their line in chic beachwear.

We head for the car park, still sweating cobs in our unsuitable gear, when we see one of those small souvenir shops which stock all things seaside.

'Look,' I say excitedly. 'We might get something to wear in there!'

'Such as?' says DB, who is not sharing my enthusiasm. 'A snorkel? Flippers? A stick of rock?'

Nevertheless, I venture in, and there, folded into a small pile, are some t-shirts! I give them only a cursory glance, more intent on finding the right sizes. Luckily, I find two that will fit and return to DB triumphant at my find.

Back at the apartment, we're ready to hit the beach again.

'Right, let's get these t-shirts on,' I say, 'we'll show those scoffers who thought we were dressed like crackpots this morning.'

We don the t-shirts and look at ourselves in the mirror. There before us, according to the slogans emblazoned on our chests, stands a decrepit 'SURFER DUDE' accompanied by a pre-historic 'BEACH BABE'! Not sure what the locals are going to make of that, but safe to say they won't be changing their opinion that we're a total pair of nutters.

ON THE ROAD AGAIN

So, the Bundells are 'oop north' touring Northumberland, my childhood stamping ground. We've invested in a new car with multiple bells and whistles, which includes an EXTREMELY annoying sat nav lady who we've christened Doreen.

Now, it could be that Doreen is so sophisticated that she can sense there are two old duffers in the car, and one of them is a bit Mutt and Jeff, but something is making her repeat everything at least twice, maybe in the hope that it will eventually sink in. Roundabouts particularly annoy her. 'Take the second exit, the second exit, turn at the SECOND exit,' she declaims in a bossy voice. She stops short of 'How many times do I have to tell you!' but only just.

At a bit of a tricky junction, I miss the turning and send her apoplectic. 'Take the first left, the first left, the first...., do a U-turn and take the first right, the first right, turn right, turn right onto the A1, THE A1!' she shouts. By this time, a new car or not, I'm ready to rip the sat nav out of the dashboard and chuck it out the window.

We decide to visit Cragside, the beautiful stately home not far from the hotel. 'Shouldn't we book dinner before we leave?' suggests DB.

'No need,' I say airily. 'It's a Tuesday, they won't be busy.'

We set off to find the house despite Doreen, who is obviously still finding her bearings, sending us a) along a farm track, b) into someone's drive, and c) up a No Entry.

We spend a good few hours looking round the house and walking through the lovely gardens, so by the time we stop for lunch, it is almost 2 o'clock. DB is ravenous (nothing unusual there!).

'Let's get some lunch,' he says.

'I'll just have a quick look in the gift shop,' I reply breezily. 'Won't be a mo.'

DB is not impressed. 'You've got ten minutes,' he harrumphs.

Half an hour later I emerge to find DB pacing up and down, about to mug a small child eating a packet of crisps.

I hurry him to the cafe only to find that the coach load of OAP's we saw earlier, has gone through the sandwiches like a plague of locusts.

'Brilliant!' says DB, somewhat sarcastically in my estimation, as he surveys a couple of dried-out scones that are left.

Still, it's food, so we eat them, consoling ourselves with the thought of the four-course dinner we'll have later that evening.

As we arrive back at the hotel, DB says, 'I'm absolutely famished. Let's have dinner early tonight.'

'Good idea,' I say and ask the receptionist if we can book a table for half past six.

'Sorry,' she says as she surveys the bookings, 'our first available table is 8.30. You should have booked earlier.'

I daren't look at DB, but I can sense his blood pressure is at boiling point.

'Thank you,' I say sweetly and beat it before murder is done.

***

Today, we visited Lindisfarne and Bamborough Castle. Lindisfarne went without incident, except that for the first time in 400 years, it's undergoing repairs and is covered in scaffolding! Natch—wouldn't have expected anything else with our track record!

I can hear the National Trust discussion now...

'We really need to repair Lindisfarne and cover it in scaffolding. When would be a good time?'

'Well, the Bundells are here in July.'

'July it is then.'

Later, we visit Bamborough Castle. All is going swimmingly, blue skies, warm sunshine, and not a scaffolding pole in sight, when we're joined by a very loud man and his two friends. He has obviously appointed himself tour guide for the group and reads out every little detail in the guidebook in a deafening voice like some kind of Geordie Darth Vader.

'THIS IS THE GREAT KITCHEN,' he booms. 'NOTE THE THREE FIREPLACES ON THE FAR WALL,' he roars.

He continues in this vein, and as anyone with a guidebook has just read this for themselves, he's soon in danger of being gagged by a crowd of hacked-off tourists.

'THIS NEXT ROOM IS THE KING'S HALL,' he thunders. I'm flicking through my guidebook, doing my best not to throttle him with my bare hands, when he walks over and says,

'WE'RE ON PAGE 10, PET.'

I smile through gritted teeth and thank him even though I'm on page 10 anyway.

In the next room, which is the billiards room, I'm looking around when he says, 'I THINK YOU'LL FIND THIS IS THE GREAT DINING ROOM, PET.'

'No, this is the billiards room,' I reply.

'NO PET, YOU MUST BE ON THE WRONG PAGE AGAIN,' he insists. 'IT'S THE GREAT DINING ROOM.'

Now I know I'm not the most observant of people, but even I have noticed the flaming enormous billiards table which takes up most of the room.

'Isn't that a billiards table?' I ask pointedly. 'That probably means this is the billiards room,' I continue, sounding just the tiniest bit sarky.

He looks at the table as if to say, who put that there, flicks through his guidebook to check if I'm right, and then, with the wind well and truly taken out of his sails, he shuts up and continues on his way. Result!

At the end of our tour, we're just about to head for the tearoom when we hear a familiar booming voice say to his friends, 'LET'S GET A CUP OF TEA.'

DB and I look at each other with dread, turn tail, and beat a hasty path back to the car.

***

It's 4 am the following morning, and I'm awoken by a noise. The bedroom window is rattling annoyingly in the wind. I nudge DB, who, as usual, is snoring and blissfully unaware of anything amiss.

'Wake up,' I whisper.

Nothing.

A more forceful nudge. 'Wake up.'

The snoring continues.

I give him a good shake, 'Yoo hoo, sleeping beauty!'

'What? What is it?' DB wakes with a start.

'It's windy,' I say.

'Told you not to have the cabbage,' he mutters, still half asleep.

'No! Outside! It's windy outside.'

'And?'

'The windows are rattling.'

'And?'

'Someone needs to close them.'

'Go on then,' he says and turns over.

I elbow him in the ribs. 'Not me, you!'

'Why?'

'It's a man's job to close windows in the middle of the night.'

'Why?'

'Because that's what men do. Same as taking the bins out.'

Too tired to follow my twisted logic, he gives in and staggers out of bed, muttering, 'Yes, your ladyship, whatever you say, your ladyship.'

Satisfied that the problem is solved, I ignore him and instantly fall asleep again.

Now, unfortunately, DB must negotiate the tea table and then two pairs of full-length velvet curtains to get to the bay windows, which are old and stiff and take a bit of persuasion before they close.

It takes a few minutes, but mission accomplished, he turns towards bed again—only to find he's completely entangled in the heavy, voluminous curtains.

Assuming he is back under the duvet by now, I come to, to hear my name being called in a ghostly whisper, 'Fiona! Fiona!'

I jump up in bed with a shock to see, in the half-light, the curtains moving on their own, accompanied by the ghostly rattle of teacups.

By now, I'm ready to scream the place down. My heart is thumping, and I go to wake DB again and realise he's not there.

'Fiona! Fiona!' I hear again emanating from nowhere. Groggy with sleep, I'm convinced a ghost has spirited DB to the hereafter, and now it's coming for me! I'm just about to crack the entity over the head with the bedside lamp when I hear,

'Get me out; I'm stuck in the curtains!'

Realising it's my darling (said sarcastically) husband, I snap on the light and disentangle him.

'For pity's sake, what are you doing? You scared the living daylights out of me!' I hiss, aware that anything louder might wake the couple in the next room.

94

'I didn't do it on purpose,' he hisses back.

It's too difficult to conduct a marital tiff in the middle of the night in sibilant stage whispers so I climb back into bed and, as just punishment in my book, I make sure I've got most of the duvet.

***

This morning, Doreen completely loses her marbles. We leave our hotel in Northumberland to travel to another hotel in Yorkshire for a couple of nights. We're travelling on the A1. We know it's the A1 because all the signs say it's the A1. The map book says it's the A1. But not Doreen. Doreen's screen shows us to be in the middle of a random field somewhere, and she's telling us, over and over again, in her own mind-numbing fashion, that she is 'Recalculating, Recalculating, Recalc...' well, you get the gist.

If this isn't bad enough, an hour later, she insists, 'You have reached your destination,' when clearly, we are nowhere near it unless the hotel is invisible and situated in the middle of a country lane somewhere.

Is it because the car is Japanese? Should we be reading the sat nav from right to left? Is her insistence on repeating the same thing over and over again a new form of Japanese water torture? Whatever it is, she better sort herself out or it will soon be 'sayonara' Doreen.

***

Dinner was interesting tonight! We arrive at the hotel restaurant and are told that our waitress will be with us shortly. Eventually, a waitress, who probably last served on the Titanic, begins to weave her way very slowly and unsteadily towards us. She is a dead ringer for the doddery old waitress in the 'Two Soups' sketch by Victoria Wood, bent over like a question mark with slightly baggy tights and an overly long apron.

'Bread roll, madam?' she asks in a quavering voice.

'Yes, please,' I say.

Just like the waitress in the sketch, anything she holds gradually but inexorably heads downwards. The breadbasket lists dangerously, and a bread roll makes for my lap. I catch it and put it on my plate.

'Well caught, madam!' she says, not the least embarrassed that she's the one who dropped it.

Turning to go, her balance, clearly dodgy, makes her teeter dangerously on a collision course for the neighbouring table. But all is not lost. At the last moment, she executes an obviously well-practiced sort of sideways canter and manages to steer herself back on a straight path.

A few minutes later, she returns with a jug of water.

'Water, madam?'

Her hand is shaking so violently I can hardly hear her over the noise of ice cubes clanking against the glass jug.

DB and I look at one another in alarm. Is she kidding?

'Er, just a little,' I stupidly hear myself say.

I prepare myself for a drenching, but by some miracle, it's only the tablecloth that suffers.

'And you, sir?'

DB, mindful of his best shirt, wisely declines.

Two minutes later, she's back with the breadbasket again.

'Bread roll, madam?' she says, oblivious to the fact she's only just asked us.

'We've had one thank you,' I say.

She looks momentarily nonplussed, then adeptly covering her senior moment, insists, 'Yes, but they're so delicious, you must have another,' and as if to compensate for her mistake, she continues, 'In fact, have two,' and plops them on our plates.

We now have three rolls each and a very damp tablecloth.

We look at the menu.

'For Pete's sake, don't order the soup!' DB says out of the corner of his mouth.

Mindful of her tremor, we look for the least slippery food we can find on the menu.

She returns with her pad, and we give her our order.

'I'll have the asparagus please,' I say.

'Yes, madam, the a-spa-ra-gus,' she repeats slowly and takes the next five minutes to write it down.

'And for main course, madam?'

'I'll have the fish,' I say, thinking this would take less time to write down than 'salmon en croûte'.

'The fish, madam,' she repeats, but she is not going to be hurried and painstakingly articulates, 'That would be the sal-mon-en-cro-ute, madam.'

This takes so long that we contemplate giving up on dinner and ordering breakfast instead.

Five minutes later, she begins to head our way with the breadbasket again.

'Oh blimey, here comes more bread,' I whisper.

'Strewth! I've got more rolls here than Hovis,' grumbles DB. 'Be firm. Tell her we don't want one.'

I'm just about to break the bad news when she catches sight of our plates, sees they're already laden with rolls, and realises her mistake. She does another doddery turn, lurches back to the side table with the breadbasket, and picks up the water jug again.

My heart sinks. This is like being on Groundhog Day. But, phew, she makes her way towards two other unsuspecting diners to christen their tablecloth.

The management, mindful of the laundry bills that would ensue if she was allowed to serve any actual food, have obviously appointed another team of waitresses to do this because a youngster arrives, and we are served the rest of the meal without incident. But as we leave the restaurant, there she is again, bent over a new table of diners with her wayward breadbasket.

'Bread roll, madam?'

RAINDROPS KEEP FALLING ON MY HEAD....

The Bundells are in Amsterdam for a few days. We've been under leaden skies for most of the Eurostar journey, so when we arrive at Centraal Station, it's good to see a glimmer of sun. A ten-second glimmer of sun, to be precise, because this is the Bundells—the same Bundells who once holidayed in sunny California and had two days of sunshine in three weeks!

Just as we step foot outside, the rain Gods clock us and have a quick confab along the lines of, 'Look, lads, it's the Bundells; let 'em have it with both barrels!' The heavens open, and rain lashes down like stair rods.

'Quick, get your umbrella out!' DB shouts, ignoring the fact I'm trundling a heavy case in one hand and a bulky hold-all in the other. I wrestle the umbrella out of my bag, but by then, a pair of drowned rats would look positively desiccated in comparison to us.

'Let's get a taxi,' I say, dripping water, but no, DB wants an 'adventure,' so we buy tickets for the tram.

'Travel cards are automated here,' says the information desk lady. 'Just tap your pass in and out on the tram,' she explains.

My heart sinks at the dreaded word 'automated.' It's the stuff of nightmares, as far as I'm concerned. In my time, I've single-handedly brought both the Paris metro and the Hermitage in St Petersburg to a complete standstill because of automated ticket barriers.

The tram arrives, and we get on board, with me now juggling a case, a hold-all, an umbrella, AND a tram card. DB abandons me (what's new) to find a seat as I try to beat the luggage into submission while at the same time tapping in with the tram card. All is going well until the umbrella turns bolshie and decides to jam itself between the closing tram doors.

'Now, what do I do?' I think. I've got half an umbrella inside the tram and half outside, a hold-all on my shoulder, and a case on wheels that has gone rogue and is making a beeline for the kneecaps of an unsuspecting Amsterdam citizen.

Do I let go of the umbrella to rescue the case? Or use both hands to free the brolly, let the case freelance, and risk inflicting GBH on an elderly Dutchman?

DB, whose rain-splattered glasses have only just de-misted, at last sees my dilemma and niftily sticks out one of his size 11s, which thankfully stops the case in its tracks.

Eventually, it dawns on the gormless doors that something is jamming them, so they shoot open again, just as I try to free the umbrella with an almighty yank. DB, still keeping the suitcase at bay with his foot, watches with horror as me, the hold-all, and the umbrella are all propelled backward into the lap of the man sitting opposite.

Apologising profusely, I stand up to see an entire busload of Amsterdammers looking on in total bemusement.

I'd like to act nonchalant, but it's difficult when you've just outdone Norman Wisdom in the slapstick stakes, so head bowed in embarrassment, I squelch my way to a vacant seat and resolve that the next time DB wants an 'adventure', I'm heading in the opposite direction.

***

We decide to go to the very popular Rijksmuseum the following day, so DB insists that we get up early to beat the queues.

'No need,' I explain rather smugly. 'I've downloaded this clever app on my phone, which means all we have to do is show a barcode, and hey presto, we're in!'

'You're not trusting anything on that interweb, are you?' says DB, the world's worst technophobe.

'Look, you've got to get down with the kids! Get into the 21st century, bruv,' I say, but he's not listening as he sets his alarm on 'crack of dawn' setting.

The next morning, bleary-eyed, I stagger down to breakfast.

'A Trappist monk wouldn't be up this early,' I grumble, but DB has gone selectively deaf again.

We catch the tram at Centraal station and arrive at the museum even before the milk's been delivered; but give DB his due, there is hardly anyone here, so we walk straight up to the ticket barrier. I present my phone, thinking, 'Ooh, get me with the paperless technology!' and the guide zaps it with his machine.

Nothing. No bleep. No ping. No ting. Nothing.

'Sorry, madam,' he says, 'it doesn't seem to be working,'

'But it must be,' I insist, jabbing the screen with an angry finger. 'I downloaded it!'

'Told you,' mutters DB under his breath.

I'm tempted to ram the mobile phone down someone's throat, anyone's throat, but knew if I did, we'd never get in.

I ask the guide to try again. He does.

Nothing. Not a dicky bird.

'Wait!' I say as I remember that I'd done a belt and braces, and pull out a paper copy of the pass and show it to him with a flourish.

'See, this document proves it!'

The guide reads it and then points to the dreaded small print, which says that the bar code has to be presented to the central office for verification before it can be used.

'Oh, that's no problem!' I say, only just restraining myself from sticking my tongue out triumphantly at DB.

'And where is the office?' I ask, looking around me to see if it's nearby.

'Across the other side of town,' he replies. And then, as I look blank. 'Near Centraal Station.'

Bummer! We've only just come from there!

'What did I say about trusting technology!' DB says, exulting in his moment of victory.

We scramble on another tram, arrive at the office, get the code verified, come back on yet ANOTHER tram, and return to the museum.

Yep. The place is heaving. We can't move for tourists, school parties, art students—it's a blooming nightmare.

'Good job we got up early,' I say.

DB's face says it all.

***

The rain Gods are still putting us through the wringer, so to speak, which is no bad thing, because it's been raining for three solid days. It's so consistently wet there's obviously some serious Ark building going on somewhere.

DB and I have exhausted most of the indoor museums, so I'm scouting the guidebook for options to stay dry.

'What else can we do that means we won't get wet?' I ask. 'My pac-a-mac is about to ring Samaritans—it can't take any more.'

'I know what we can do,' says DB. 'If we catch a Hop on Hop off bus, we'll see some more of the tourist sites AND stay dry!'

'Yeh, sorry to put a dampener on things,' I pun, somewhat wittily in my opinion, 'but see that red dot in the distance? That's the bus, and the next one's not due for half an hour!'

'Never mind,' he says, 'look, there's a cafe over there. We can sit in it until the bus comes.'

I look at where he's pointing.

'Er, I don't think so,' I warn.

'Why not?' says DB, who is licking his lips in anticipation of a large piece of apple pie.

'It's not a cafe,' I say.

He looks at me as if I've lost my mind.

'Of course, it's a cafe!' he exclaims. 'Look, it says CO-FF-EE SH-OP in huge letters!' he points out, slowly enunciating every syllable in case I'd lost grasp of the English language.

'Yes, but it's not THAT kind of coffee shop,' I say and wink dramatically.

DB looks perplexed.

'You know! It's where they sell 'special' cake!' I repeat and wink dramatically again.

'Great,' DB says, 'I like cake, and by the way, there's something wrong with your eye.'

'No!!' I shout, getting more and more exasperated. 'It's one of THOSE places. You know where naughty things are on sale!'

'Wait, what? Is this the red-light district, then? I thought the girls stood in a window.' He peers at the coffee shop with its two tiny windows. 'They're going to have to be contortionists to fit in there!'

There's a slight pause.

'Come to think of it....,'

'Noooooo!' I interrupt quickly before the conversation gets any more lurid. 'It's where cannabis is sold—they're called coffee shops.'

'Stupid blooming name to call them if they don't sell coffee.... Or cake,' he says crestfallen, as the expectation of a slice of pie melts into oblivion.

We stand in the pouring rain, and at last, the bus arrives.

'Come on,' I say as we clamber on board. 'Let's enjoy this. It's our last chance to see some more of Amsterdam before we go home.'

If only! We sit down ready to enjoy our last trip, but the rain has completely steamed up not only the bus windows, but also DB's glasses.

'Marvellous!' he says. 'Can't see a blooming thing!'

The commentary points out all the wonderful sights of Amsterdam as we pass them, but looking through the fogged-up windows with two pairs of fogged-up glasses, we might as well be on a bus tour through Dartford! The rain Gods have had the last laugh.

ROAMIN' IN THE GLOAMIN'

We've long wanted to do a road trip round the NC500, which is the road that skirts the very north of Scotland, so we travel to Inverness by train and then intend to drive the rest of the way, stopping off on route.

Determined to make an early start, we leave the hotel immediately after breakfast to pick up the hire car I'd found on a good deal online.

'Thrifty Car Hire, please,' I say to the cab driver, trying to ignore the fact that the name isn't filling me with confidence.

'Thrifty?' he says. 'Thrifty? Are ye sure? I've no' heard o' them.'

'I told you it sounded dodgy,' grumbles DB, who always thinks my 'deals' are suspect. 'Probably next to "Inverness Rent-a-Wreck",' he continues.

We eventually find it, and when the paperwork is finished, they go to fetch the car.

DB continues to be sceptical.

'Thrifty Car Hire? You wait, it'll have 3 wheels and no hand brake,' he mutters and then does a double take as a BMW draws up outside.

DB is suddenly looking nervous. 'Blimey, is that it? I better not prang that,' he says, contemplating the nasty hairpin bends that make up the road for the next 500 miles.

We set off with my Dearly Beloved in a muck sweat and are not 10 miles down the road when suddenly there is a huge CRACK! At first, we're confused (ok, it doesn't take a lot these days), and then we both look on in horror as a large chip begins to spreadeagle itself across the windscreen.

AAAAARGH!

Neither of us can believe it. We phone the car hire firm who tell us that we have to return the car. So, we begin the drive back, bemoaning our bad luck.

'Actually,' says DB chirpily, 'I'm quite relieved; I'll feel much more relaxed driving a less expensive car than a BMW on those single-track roads. A Ford Focus would suit me much better.'

'Don't worry,' I say cheerily, 'When they see what's happened, you'll be lucky to get a scooter.'

We arrive at the garage and begin another mountain of paperwork. The bad news is that a BMW windscreen with sensors/ heating elements and other fancy-schmancy gizmos will cost £450 to replace. Gulp!

'It could be worse,' I say in an attempt to cheer DB up, 'the insurance will probably cover it, and at least you'll feel more relaxed driving something smaller.'

The car hire lady returns. 'That's all the paperwork done, and I've got a bit of good news for you… as all our smaller cars are out, we're giving you something bigger.' We look out of the car hire window, and DB's face takes on a deathly pallor. 'It's a Jag!' he gulps.

'I knew you'd be pleased,' she says, not realising that she's just totally ruined DB's holiday.

I prepare myself to be driven at a top speed of 10 miles an hour for the rest of the trip.

***

So, after a long (and extremely slow!) drive, we arrive at our first B&B. It's in the back-of-beyond along an endlessly twisting single-track road, populated by jaywalking sheep who seriously need to brush up their green cross code.

Now, when I made the booking, it was the only accommodation available in the area, so I 'inadvertently forgot' to tell DB that it's a vegetarian establishment.

On arrival, DB settles down to read the info in the room. I wait for the inevitable reaction. But not for long.

'What the...! Have you seen this?' he jumps up in alarm, stabbing his finger furiously at the words 'vegetarian breakfast'.

'Er, yes, dear,' I say, avoiding his eye.

'Vegetarian! Vegetarian!! I don't believe it!' DB splutters, channelling his inner Victor Meldrew again.

Now it's a fact that DB's carnivore tendencies are matched only by Desperate Dan of 'Beano' fame, so he is not a happy camper.

'Well, we're not staying here for dinner,' he says in a tone that brooks no argument.

'But the nearest restaurant is miles away,' I remind him, 'along that dreadful road with the suicidal sheep.'

But DB, already bereft at the thought of his brekkie with no bangers, refuses to face the possibility of a nut cutlet for dinner, so he insists that we drive back along the twisting road to the nearest restaurant that can provide him with some meat!

I can only pray that the quest is successful, or those sheep will be lamb chops if DB has his way!

***

There's nothing DB likes more than a long hot shower in the mornings, so the fact our next B&B has one of those swanky rain shower heads is a big step up from our last place—the one run by two cranky vegetarian eco-warriors dressed in full 'care in the community' guise, who'd have much preferred us to have a quick rub down with yesterday's newspaper than use any of their precious water!

So, this morning I wait for DB to finish luxuriating in the shower...and wait...and wait. Finally, impatience wins.

'What are you doing in there?' I shout through the door. 'Hurry up!'

'It's ok, Keep the heid,' says DB, who's picked up some of the local vernacular, and opens the bathroom door.

He's been in there so long I can barely see him through the clouds of steam that billow out of the bathroom. I'm just cleaning my teeth when all hell lets loose. The steam has set off the smoke alarm!

DB looks aghast and dashes out to try and stop it. I decide to help and am met by the ridiculous sight of DB dressed in only a towel, desperately trying to waft the steam away by jumping up and down and, at the same time, madly whirling a flannel above his head. He's a dead ringer for some semi-naked, demented Morris dancer, and I crease up.

'Don't just stand there laughing,' DB shouts, 'get wafting before a flaming fire engine turns up!' After a couple of minutes of synchronised wafting, the alarm stops, and we breathe a sigh of relief.

'Blimey, I'm sweating!' says DB exhausted by all the exertion. 'I need another shower.'

'Don't even think about it!' I exclaim, locking the bathroom door firmly behind me.

***

We're in Skye on what is billed as 'A magical boat trip to Loch Coruisk'. We sail past the magnificent Cuillin mountains, distant misty islands, and basking seals before beginning our walk to the Loch. Now, if clambering over mountainous rocks and dodging boggy quagmires is your thing, you'd love it. Me? I'm not so sure that it's ideal for two not-so-spring chickens, but I soldier on.

It's soon clear that my Brownie badge for rambling isn't going to cut it, and I suggest we turn back and wait for the boat to return. But not DB, oh no! He's in full Bear Grylls mode by now, on a mission, in it for the long haul.

Now my brand-new trainers are not waterproof (I know, I despair of myself sometimes) and the ground is becoming more and more boggy.

'Look, it's all right for you with your dirty great hiking boots on, but I'm going to get wet feet,' I complain.

'Come on, don't be such a wuss!' DB says, encouragement never being one of his fortes.

Not far on, the bog has turned into a veritable swamp— one that's just daring you to put a foot wrong. I view it with trepidation.

'Right, that's it, I'm turning back.'

But DB refuses to be beaten and, with a bit of nifty footwork, reaches the other side.

'Come on,' he says. 'I'll help you. Just put your foot on that rock in the middle, and you'll be fine.'

'What rock in the middle?'

'That one,' he points.

I take a leap.

'No, not that one!' DB shouts, but too late. SQUELCH. One foot sinks into the mire, followed by the other one. I watch with horror as my brand-new trainers become engulfed with goo, and icy water seeps through to my feet.

DB, for some reason, finds this terribly amusing.

'You should see the look on your face!' he guffaws.

I turn and make my way back trying to keep some semblance of dignity despite making rude slurping noises with every step.

'Ha, ha, you've properly put your foot in it now!' DB shouts after me, amused at his own joke.

'I know EXACTLY where I'd like to put my foot!' I mutter and continue on my way.

Back at the landing dock, I find a flattish rock, take off my socks and shoes, and break the news to DB that, heart condition or no heart condition, if the boat arrives before they're dry, a piggyback is on the cards.

That wipes the smile off his face.

SUN, SEA, AND (A LOT OF) SAND

We're in Fuerteventura, one of the Canary Islands.

'Let's go for a walk and see the sand dunes,' I say. 'The guidebook says they're magnificent, just like a proper desert.'

That did it. Cue my Dearly Beloved in full Lawrence of Arabia mode. He begins poring over the map, plots a course, and oddly, in my humble opinion, marks the only garage for miles with a large red cross. 'Er, what's that for?' I say, 'Don't think a gentle stroll to the sand dunes necessitates much petrol.'

DB looks at me witheringly, 'To stock up on water, of course. This is serious stuff! We're walking in 30 degrees of heat; dehydration is a real concern.'

I'm a bit worried that it seems we're going to walk ACROSS the dunes and not TO the dunes, which was my preferred option, but, hey ho, what can possibly go wrong! 'Ok, Lawrence,' I say sarcastically. 'Would you care to don a hotel sheet and tea towel? You know, just so you can look the part? Do the full Peter O'Toole?'

No reply.

So, we set off. After we've been walking for about an hour on sandy scrubland, I look at the makeshift map that the hotel has given us.

'We need to turn left here,' I say.

'No, it's right,' says DB, peering into the distance like a fully paid-up Bedouin.

'Are you sure?' I query, always wary of DB's dodgy sense of direction.

Another withering look comes my way. We turn right.

An hour later, I have half the Sahara in each shoe, multiple leg lacerations from desert scrub, and with no sign of the garage watering hole, I'm seriously considering sucking the heck out of a packet of Wet Ones.

And do we see the dunes by turning right?

One. We see one. The rest lie in the opposite direction! That would be LEFT!

So, dunes—or should I say, dune—walked, the beach beckons. Walking across the sand hand in hand, barefoot, is quite romantic in its way—though the random thought that I may never need to exfoliate my feet again rather spoils the mood.

'Here's a spot,' says DB, ready to lay down his towel, but I had spotted a much quieter bit further away.

'No, let's keep walking, there's hardly anyone over there.'

Off I set, wind in my ears, semi-blinded by the brilliant white sand. In the distance, I think I can vaguely hear DB shouting, 'Noooo! This way!'

'Follow your directions again? No way!' I mutter and stride on. Head down, I almost trip over a recumbent sunbather.

'Sorry!' I apologise. Then I realise why DB had been shouting... I have stumbled across, and I mean LITERALLY stumbled across, the nudist beach. I avert my eyes but, too late—the image is seared into my brain. Suffering a touch of PTSD, I need a lie down with some smelling salts but decide the best course of action is to get the heck out of there pronto, so I scamper back across the sand to where DB is waiting. I can't help wondering if his smug smile has anything to do with his satisfaction that, this time, it is my bad!

***

Later that day, I say, 'Let's go into town for some presents to take back with us.'

'That's not an excuse to go dress shopping, is it!' DB says suspiciously, his 'I hate shopping' antennae twitching.

'Nuhhnnnnmm,' I mutter in a non-committal way.

Having done enough walking today and being aware of the afternoon heat, I suggest a taxi, but DB's having none of it.

So, we walk.

We walk 3 miles... In 30 degrees of heat.

But I have my revenge, as somehow, we arrive at a dress shop (hmm, how did that happen?). Hot and somewhat sweaty, I spy a lovely dress and go into the changing room while the long-suffering DB waits outside.

'This is a bit big,' I shout through the curtain. 'Can you get me a size Small?'

'A Small?' DB splutters in disbelief. 'Really?'

My turn to give a withering look.

But the day's dilemmas are not over yet. Small goes on a treat. Small doesn't come off a treat. Hot, damp skin means Small is well and truly stuck over my shoulders.

'Psssst! You'll have to help me,' I hiss through the curtain.

DB sighs. Deeply.

It rapidly becomes evident that the half-hearted tugging on his part through the curtain isn't cutting it. He needs to come inside. There is much grunting and giggling, and then, just as he manages to tug the dress over my head, everything stops, and I am temporarily blinded.

In his best broken English, I hear, 'It eez ok. This lady she eez wife.'

I emerge with one last tug to see that a shocked shop assistant, wondering what on earth was happening, has swept aside the changing room curtain. The poor woman is clearly traumatised by the grisly sight of an overheated OAP dragging the clothes off a red-faced, sweaty woman, so we leave the shop 'rapidamente' before the police are called. Just as well it is the last day of the holiday. Interpol will never catch us.

A FLORIDA ROAD TRIP

We are off to a flying—or not-so-flying start (courtesy of Virgin Airlines) to our Florida road trip. We've boarded, but that's it. Nothing else seems to be happening. It goes something like this…

1. The co-pilot, at the last minute, pulls a sickie.

2. Wait an hour and a half while a replacement is found.

3. Spend time nervously remembering the co-pilot in the film 'Airplane.'

4. Keep our eyes peeled for any blow-up dolls entering the cockpit.

5. Wait even longer because now the co-pilot's luggage has gone AWOL.

6. Seriously consider a whip round to buy him a toothbrush and some PJs.

7. Plane eventually takes off.

8. My pre-ordered meal doesn't materialise.

9. Face the prospect of a 10-hour flight with no food.

10. DB, unconcerned, tucks into his chicken tikka masala with relish.

Dare I say this is 'Virgin' on the ridiculous!

***

We eventually arrive at our hotel in the beautiful Florida Keys. There is a long veranda outside the bedrooms, which is like a thoroughfare in front of all the rooms. It's a lovely spot to sit at night and listen to the sea. So tonight, feeling jet lagged and hot, I decide to get into my PJs early and sit here for a mo' and watch the waves.

'What on earth are you doing?' asks DB, as he sees me opening the door in my pyjamas. Well, not an ACTUAL door in my pyjamas, that would be silly, the door to the...well, you know what I mean.

'It's ok,' I reassure him, 'Everyone's still at dinner.'

DB looks at me as if I'd gone loopy. 'But you're in your pyjamas!' he splutters.

'It doesn't matter, no one will see me.'

Reluctantly, he comes out to sit with me. Moments later, there is a strong gust of wind, and the door slams shut, locking us out of our room.

'Great!' exclaims DB, 'Now I'll have to go to reception and get another key.'

He is gone some time while I sit on the veranda, trying to look as inconspicuous as any old biddy can, who is sitting in her pyjamas in a public place. DB returns, looking grumpy. 'There's no one at reception,' he says. 'So, we'll just have to wait here.'

As time passes, people begin to return from dinner to their rooms. Their furtive looks and hidden smirks say it all.

'Don't worry,' I say to DB who is looking a tad embarrassed. 'Just pretend to be my Carer.'

DB just shakes his head in disbelief.

***

The next day, I lose my sunglasses. We have just left the Dolphin Centre when I realise they're gone. They aren't in my bag; they aren't in the car; they aren't anywhere. These are prescription sunglasses that have cost me an arm and several legs and I am now in a panic. Then I realise I must have left them in the Dolphin Centre. By now, DB has gone to dry off, so I set off to find the trainer, who is now having lunch.

'Sorry to disturb your lunch,' I say, 'but I've left my sunglasses here. Could I look for them?'

'Sure, ma'am,' she says with barely a glance, much more interested in her phone while she scoffs her pastrami on rye.

I look everywhere. Nothing. Not a sign of them. Despondent, I return to the trainer's office.

'No, can't find them anywhere,' I tell her.

The trainer looks up.

'What do they look like, ma'am?'

'Well, they've got sort of purple frames,' I say.

There is a pause.

'Would they be the ones on your head?' she asks in the same voice you'd use to humour a five-year-old.

Oh dear, another senior moment.

'I'm so sorry,' I apologise in total embarrassment.

'No praa-blem,' she drawls, while in reality thinking, 'Lady, you should be put in a home.'

She returns to her pastrami on rye.

I return to DB to try and explain this one away.

***

So those mad enough to follow the crazy ramblings of the Bundells on holiday might remember the debacle of the 3-mile walk in the searing heat of Fuerteventura. Well, it's happened again.

DB decides a walk to the pier for elevenses would be good, so despite my better judgement—it's blooming hot by that time of the morning—we set off. Gasping my last but staving off collapse with the thought of a nice cool drink when we get there, we turn the corner and find the sign— PIER CLOSED! Fabulous, just what I need! Now we have to walk another couple of miles back before there is any sign of a cafe. I also desperately need the loo, but then figure even if I find one, I daren't use it as I need to hang on to any drop of moisture I can!

DB, in denial mode, says I'll be fine when I mention I might pass out with heat stroke at any minute. 'You've had something to drink this morning,' he says.

'Yes, a cup of tea and a sip of water to take a tablet with,' I remind him. His answer?

'A camel could last all day on that!'

Well, I may not be a camel, but I've most certainly got the hump! Never again! But then I said that last time!

***

'Let's go to Sanibel today,' I say, 'the guidebook says it's lovely.'

'Yeh, great idea,' says DB with a broad smile. 'What's there?'

'A beach.'

The smile on DB's face disappears faster than a Floridian hurricane.

'A beach? With sand?'

'Er, yes.'

'I hate sand. It gets in your socks, in your shoes, in between your toes.'

'Not if you wear flip-flops.'

'Flip flops? I hate flip-flops! They're uncomfortable. They don't stay on your feet. They're instruments of torture!'

'You'll be fine,' I say, throwing his flip-flops into the back of the car.

An hour later, we're walking along the beautiful white beach at Sanibel.

DB limps along behind me, stopping every few minutes to vigorously shake alternate legs in an effort to shift the sand out of his flip-flops while at the same time swatting the sand flies away with his handkerchief. It's a strange sight—rather like a bad hokey-cokey being performed by a deranged Morris man, but hey, ho, that's DB for you.

We eventually head back to the car, and now DB faces the dilemma of how best to brush the sand from his feet. He balances one buttock on the ridge of the open boot and tries to hitch up his other foot.

DB's face gets redder and redder. Effort or anger? It's hard to tell.

There is much grunting and grimacing and a fair bit of muttering about the probability of groin injuries and hernias. My giggling doesn't seem to help.

At last, the feat (or feet) is done. 'Ok, where to now?' asks DB.

I mull it over. *Back to the hotel or......?*

The memory of being made to walk miles in the heat to a non-existent pier helps me decide.

'Captiva's not far,' I say.

'Ok, what's there?'

'A beach.'

DB stops in his tracks, and rivalling John McEnroe, yells. 'You can-not be serious!'

Revenge is sweet!

***

We've discovered there are a number of problems in doing a road trip when one is no longer in the first flush of youth. One of them is remembering what your room number is. We just get one room number into our brains when we move on; there is a new town, a new hotel, a new room, and a new room number.

DB has been found trying to ram one of those credit card key thingies into the wrong slot on more than one occasion. However, the hotel we're currently staying in has the answer! Each room has a number and a picture! So much easier to remember you're in Daisies than 425!

And what's the name of the hotel with this brilliant idea? Don't ask me. Can't remember!

***

Today, DB obliterates 20 billion dollars' worth of NASA equipment. We're visiting the Kennedy Space Centre, where simulators allow you to test your skills at landing various spacecraft. DB manages to prang 2 Atlantis space shuttles, 3

Orion capsules, and a Rover Exploration Vehicle. They ask him NOT to apply for NASA's next planned mission to Mars.

Deeply disappointed that his docking and landing skills don't pass muster, he's even more cheesed off when the 10-year-old on the next simulator completely nails it!

Sadly, it seems that DB's most likely NASA encounter will involve him wearing the T-shirt he bought in the gift shop. Shame.

***

So, sadly, our Florida Road trip has come to an end, but the mishaps continue.

We're driving to Miami airport when we spot a police car on the hard shoulder. We're well within the speed limit so all is ok. Then DB looks in his mirror. Oh, oh! Blue flashing lights mean the same in any language. We pull over. Not being hardened criminals, we are now panicking. Do we get out of the car and be seen as up for a fight, or stay put and be seen as uncooperative? Eventually, a beefy cop approaches us.

'How y'all doin' today?' he drawls.

Is that being friendly? Or American for, 'You're nicked'? I wonder.

We're told we've committed a traffic violation of not using the outside lane when passing an emergency vehicle.

127

'W-w-we're terribly sorry. We d-d-didn't know,' we stutter in unison, like two overgrown school kids.

'Driving licence, Sir,' he demands and goes off to 'check things'.

DB, remembering an ancient speeding fine he'd incurred all of 28 years ago, is convinced he'll show up on the system as wanted. He prepares himself to spend the rest of his life in Alcatraz, or whatever the modern equivalent is.

The cop returns. He looks at us for a long time. I'm mentally baking DB a cake with a large file in it. Then he says, 'Ok, Sir, as you're not a Florida resident, I'll only be issuing you a warning. You can be on your way.'

We breathe a sigh of relief. Should I kiss the cop or not? Decide, *maybe not.* DB drives the rest of the way at 10 miles an hour. In the outside lane. Just in case.

***

So, for those of you considering following in our footsteps (perhaps not our EXACT footsteps, it has to be said), here are a few hints and tips for a 3-week road trip to this lovely part of the U.S.

MAPS:

> No matter how much you spend on a road map, it will still look like it's been put through a shredder by the end of the trip.

> Be prepared to develop a permanent squint after straining your eyes for three long weeks to read the ridiculously small print on a road map.

> Learning how to unfold a road map without obscuring the entire windscreen is really useful because it means the driver isn't totally narked off all the time.

ROAD SIGNS:

> 'Pick a number, any number' is the only option when faced with the confusing variety of numbers each American road seems to have. Especially if the driver is threatening to divorce you if you don't hurry up and tell him which road he needs.

> It's potluck whether the road sign is either 2 miles or 2 inches from the turning you need. Well, that's your story, so stick to it.

> In the land of Dunkin' Donuts and Starbucks, it's Sod's law that on a three-hour journey, there isn't one to be found anywhere.

LUGGAGE:

> Pack half of what you think you'll need unless, of course, you WANT to develop arms like an orangutan from dragging a heavy suitcase around all the time.

MOTELS:

> A Motel where your fellow guests are an entire chapter of heavily tattooed, multiple-pierced Hells Angels is best avoided!

> Providing boiling water is obviously too much of a litigious risk for most motels. Be prepared for three weeks of lukewarm tea.

> If you're tempted to take home the free pen offered in every motel room you stay in, excess baggage charges become a real possibility. Don't they, DB!

> Take a fleece. Yep, it may be 80-plus degrees outside, but the air conditioning is glacial, so the likelihood of frostbite is never far away.

> Take earplugs—not just to drown out your loved one's raucous snoring, but said air conditioning is also deafening.

HUMIDITY:

> Ladies, even industrial strength conditioner will never tame the frizz fest which is now your hair. Be prepared to look like Hagrid for most of the time.

LAUNDRY:

> Learning from a previous holiday when DB's smalls, which had been drying off on our hotel balcony, took flight in a stiff breeze and landed on the balcony of an outraged woman on the floor below, I decide not to risk it again. (DB is still traumatised at having to ask for his under-crackers

back.) The answer? The hair dryer, of course. Blow dry those undies! Just a quick blast on the boxers, and you're good to go!

> Take a large tub of petroleum jelly (good for chafing caused by blow-dried underwear!).

A LIFE ON THE OCEAN WAVE

So, we are queuing on deck, waiting to disembark for the first excursion on our Baltic cruise.

'Now you're sure we've got everything,' DB asks.

'Of course,' I reply.

'You're sure?' DB says with doubt in his voice.

'Yes!' I reply grumpily. 'Passports. Check. Tickets. Check. Cruise card. Ch....'

Ah, I don't seem to have the cruise card. The cruise card that is the ONLY way you are allowed on and off the ship.

I take a deep breath, dreading DB's reaction to this piece of news.

'I seem to have lost the cruise card,' I say with a nervous giggle.

'What!' DB thunders. 'You are joking! Tell me you're joking!'

I look suitably sheepish.

'I might have left it on the breakfast table,' I venture.

'Stay there and keep our place in the queue,' DB says with a tone of exasperation in his voice. 'What floor was the restaurant on?'

'Twelve,' I say.

'What? TWELVE? That's five floors up,' DB splutters, exasperation changing into full-blown irritation.

I smile again, more sheepishly.

Some while later, DB returns red-faced and breathless.

'It's not there!'

'Perhaps someone handed into reception,' I suggest helpfully.

'And that is where?' DB is looking thunderous.

'Not sure. Floor Nine?'

DB returns some minutes later, red-faced and gasping. 'It's.' Gasp. 'Not.' Gasp. 'There.' Gasp.

I'm just about to carry out a bit of mouth-to-mouth, but seeing the other queuing passengers think better of it.

'Bloody marvellous,' he mutters, 'pay all this money for a cruise, and we're about to be incarcerated on the ruddy ship for a fortnight!'

'I'm sure I put it in here,' I say, with one more desperate scrabble in the depths of my bag.

'Oh yes, look, I did put it in here,' I say triumphantly. Here it is!

DB looks at me with murder in his eyes and the words, 'woman overboard,' running through his mind.

***

Two full days at sea have been a challenge for the slightly claustrophobic DB. He has taken to prowling the poop deck (still can't get my mind round that name!) like some manic Captain Pugwash, scanning the horizon with binoculars desperate to spot land.

I try to distract him by dragging him into the shops on board, but he soon drags me out again.......until he sees a rather natty white dinner jacket. He tries it on. His eyes mist over, and he begins humming the theme tune from 'Casablanca'.

'You must remember this: a kiss is just a kiss....'

In an instant, he has been transported into the world of his favourite movie; no longer DB, in his mind's eye, he has become Humphrey Bogart—which must make me some kind of clapped-out Ingrid Bergman, I suppose.

Pragmatic as ever, I remind him that Humph may have looked suave and sophisticated in a white DJ, but he obviously didn't share the same penchant as DB for slopping tomato soup down himself.

His bubble burst; he gives a deep sigh, takes off the jacket, and returns to the poop deck to do some more prowling.

***

If we didn't know already that cruising was for the more mature traveller, we sure know now!

134

Firstly, at the afternoon tea buffet, I just escape being mown down by a tandem of mobility scooters, driven full throttle, as they race each other to the last Bakewell slice.

Secondly, the talks on offer today say it all:

- Let's fight hair loss.

- Puffy ankles seminar

- How to cope with fallen arches

As DB would benefit from all three, I'm tempted to book him in pronto, but that means missing 'Line Dancing at a Slower Pace' with Rodeo Ryan!' Now, I'm not sure Line Dancing *can* go at a slower pace, but hey, ho, who am I to quibble?

However, our biggest mistake of the day is, after sharing a table at dinner with a pair of care home refuseniks, we take up their offer to guide us to the theatre for the evening show. We are led up so many blind alleys that we're in danger of missing not only the start of the show, but also the finale. When, at last, they declare triumphantly, 'Here we are,' we find ourselves heading for the gents' toilets!

Club 18 - 20, it is not!

P.S. St Petersburg tomorrow. Terra firma. DB is a very happy landlubber!

***

St Petersburg is a breathtaking city, elegant, ornate, and opulent.

We've been told that visiting the world-famous Hermitage will be one of the highlights of the trip, and indeed it is—but for all the wrong reasons!

DB, who is convinced that the KGB will be lurking around every corner, has already warned me to keep out of trouble. As we arrive outside the Hermitage, he pulls me aside.

'Remember, you're in Putin's Russia,' he whispers surreptitiously out of the corner of his mouth while simultaneously trying to look nonchalant.

Then, after a dramatic pause. 'Anything could happen.' He just stops short of adding, 'Mish Moneypenny', but I can tell he's in full 007 mode by now.

'Yes, James,' I reply, trying to look as if I share his crackpot ideas.

We're now at the entrance to the museum, so, trying to be helpful and keep the enormous queue moving, I spot an empty turnstile and scan my entry ticket. That's when it all goes wrong. The turnstile turns out to be exit only, so I've gummed up the works for everyone and simultaneously voided my own ticket! Our Russian guide Olga, who DB, in his paranoid fashion, has already identified as ex-KGB, launches into a tirade of Russian expletives.

'You vill hef to go through together,' she rants and gives DB and me an almighty shove towards the entrance turnstile. Well, after overindulging on cruise food for almost a week, getting DB's bottom through the turnstile is a feat in itself, let alone mine as well. We are just executing a kind of close-quarters conga when the turnstile, obviously identifying one fat bottom too many, seizes up in protest. We are completely stuck, with the rest of Russia in an ever-growing queue behind us.

This is all too much for DB, whose stress levels are now stratospheric, so cruise food to the rescue; he gives the turnstile an almighty push with his ample stomach, and we are through!

We only understand the complete mayhem behind us when we turn and see a sea of faces from all four corners of the globe waiting for 'the stupid English' (well, to be fair, the stupid Scot) to sort themselves out.

Poor, traumatised DB doesn't see much of the Hermitage after this. He is too busy wondering what the food will be like in the Siberian salt mines!

Such a shame we won't be allowed back!

***

So, we've swabbed our last deck, walked the last plank, and spliced the mainbrace a few times too many. Here are some of the things we've found out about a cruise holiday:

1. An empty hop-on/hop-off bus is never a good sign.

2. A totally out-of-sync commentary on an empty hop-on/hop-off bus should probably be expected.

3. Check which direction the empty hop-on/hop-off bus is going if you don't want your first stop to be back at the cruise terminal.

4. Screw holes look very much like a jack point on a hop-on/hop-off bus.

5. You can't hear the commentary if you plug your earphones into a screw hole.

6. People wearing dodgy knitwear are usually dreadful dinner companions.

7. If you want to see any famous tourist attraction, get there before a busload of Koreans with selfie sticks.

8. Never use an eyebrow pencil on a rolling ship unless you want to look like Groucho Marx.

You're welcome.

THE ART OF CONVERSATION

The Bundells are on the road again, exploring Krakow, so most of you are probably already shuddering at the thought of what will go wrong.

Surprisingly, there are no dramas on the way to the airport; the flight leaves on time, and DB even manages to avoid risking arrest due to the shed load of lotions and potions that he unfailingly forgets to pack in his suitcase. Even the private transfer car is waiting for us as we disembark. But then things take a turn for the worse.

Knowing not a word of Polish and the driver knowing hardly a word of English, it isn't exactly child's play to communicate exactly where the hotel is located.

'Hotel Novotel,' I say, keeping it simple.

'Tak but wheech one?' he replies.

I look at the name of the street—Zwierzyniecka—and gulp. How do you pronounce that? I give it my best shot.

'Swirzy-knicker.'

Nothing.

I try again, thinking the Z must be silent,

'Werry-necker.'

Nothing.

DB, looking over my shoulder, gives it a go.

'Schwarzenegger!' he shouts triumphantly.

'Don't be silly,' I say.

'Well, the road might be named after him,' he argues.

'Not a road in Krakow!'

'Might be. Lots of Krakens probably like Arnie's films.'

'Krakens? Krakens? Since when was Krakow populated by mythical sea creatures,' I scoff.

Meanwhile, the driver is looking bewildered by our little domestic and signals for me to show him the piece of paper that the hotel details are written on.

'Ah, tak,' he says as light dawns. 'Get in car.'

We get in the car, and some while later, we pull into a hotel driveway.

I look up at the name to see a large sign which clearly says IBIS.

Now, this would be fine, except we're not staying at an IBIS.

'Sorry, this-wrong-hotel,' I say to the driver, hoping that broken English might help communication.

'Nie, this-right-hotel,' he says with a Slavic, no-nonsense look in his eye.

'But it says IBIS,' I point out apologetically as if it is my fault the hotel has the wrong name.

'Nie, this is right hotel you want. Sat nav say so,' he insists as he unloads our luggage in a 'don't mess with me' manner. Thinking he's bound to know the city better than us, plus not wanting to create an international incident, we acquiesce and trundle our cases up to the reception desk.

'Hello, we'd like to check in,' I say. 'The name's Bundell.'

The receptionist checks her computer screen.

'Nie, we don't have a booking with that name,' she says.

Suspicion grows.

'This is the Novotel, isn't it?'

'Nie, this is IBIS,' she says, pointing at the ruddy great sign saying IBIS, while her face says, 'another stupid foreigner.'

'That's what I thought,' I say, 'but the taxi driver....' I trail off, losing the will to live, let alone try to explain it all.

'Novotel is round block. Way, way round block,' she emphasises, gesticulating repeatedly behind her.

DB and I sigh deeply. There's nothing else for it. We carry on trundling our cases 'way, way round block' until the case wheels are almost trundled to nothing.

At last, we reach the right hotel and check in. I unpack the Polish phrasebook and look up, 'You need to sack your taxi driver.'

***

Having already had trouble with the Polish language, I'm delighted that we have an English-speaking guide for our tour of the famous salt mines in Wieliczka (yeh, no clue)

We arrive at the entrance, where we meet our guide, a tiny Chinese lady.

Now, being more than a bit cloth-eared, I need to be near the guide, both to stand a chance of hearing what's being said and to lip-read. What I haven't factored in is that a salt mine, well, any mine, really, is somewhat lacking in the daylight department, which means lip reading is a non-starter. Never mind, I think, at least she speaks English, so learning about the Salt Mines will be a doddle.

Then she starts to speak. Try and imagine the accent of someone who has been brought up in China, has lived in Poland for years and is now translating Chinese/Polish into English. That.

'Harro, my name is Anna,' she says. 'I am you guy today. Welcome to the Saw Mines. We velly prow of ow rubbery Saw Mines.'

'Prees don be aflaid to ask keshton,' she continues.

I'm about to give the old hearing aids a good twiddle in case the batteries are playing up when I check with DB.

'Can you understand what she's saying?'

'Not a word,' he replies.

'I speak velly goo Engrish, so you wan know anything, jus' ask.'

By the look of bewilderment on most of our faces, I reckon her idea of 'velly good Engrish', and ours are two completely different concepts. However, we continue on our way.

The 'rubbery Saw Mines' are indeed very impressive. But, of course, the exploration of any mine means going deep underground. Do they have a lift? No. Do they have 800 steps which you have to walk down? Yes. Now, this is no problem for those with sprightly knees, but poor old DB's knees are well past their sell-by.

We wind down and down and down. And down and down and… well, you get the gist.

By the time we reach the end, DB has got as much control of his legs as Mr Blobby on a bender.

'Thank goodness, that's over,' he says as he wobbles unsteadily over to where I'm standing. 'My knees are like jelly.'

'You are now at revel one. Two mow revels to go!' Anna says.

DB can't believe his ears.

We walk down even more steps and then along 2.2 kilometres of myriad passageways, which lead to a series of breathtaking chambers. Not that DB would know, as his rubbery legs (and that's me saying that, not Anna) now have a mind of their own. Lagging severely behind, he just about manages to catch a glimpse of one chamber before Anna marches us on towards another.

'Strewth,' groans DB. 'Anna must have been in the Red Army in a former life,' he gasps. I look blank.

'The famous Long March of the Chinese Red Army?'

History not being my strong point, I continue to look blank.

'Dimwit,' he mutters into the dark.

Eventually, after two solid hours of walking, we reach the end of the tour and queue up for one of the lifts, which will take us back up to the surface.

DB, who by now has not only thrown in the towel but chucked in the entire contents of the airing cupboard, gives several deep sighs of relief, slumps against the nearest wall, energy completely spent, and waits for the lift operator to call us forward.

Suddenly, there is a very intense whispered conversation between the lift operator and Anna. She turns to us.

'So, we have to aporogise. There is something long with the rift. We ha' to walk another kirometre to neks rift.'

DB's face is murderous. Thank goodness his penknife is back at the hotel, or the ancient Chinese custom of death by a thousand cuts would have been a dead cert for Anna.

So, we've had a lovely few days in Krakow, but it's sadly time to leave. Communication hiccups seem to have been the theme of this holiday, and so it continues….

I'm waiting with the cases while DB settles the bill at reception. The taxi draws up in front of the hotel on the dot of our pickup time.

I smile at the taxi driver and give him my name, 'Fiona Bundell.'

He smiles back and says, 'Tak,' which (get me!) means yes.

'My husband is coming,' I explain. He looks rather hesitant, shrugs in a Slavic fashion, and then piles the cases into the back of the cab.

I get into the back seat and wait for DB to appear.

'Blimey, that must be some size of bill,' I think as minutes pass and he still hasn't shown up.

Suddenly, a complete stranger knocks on the cab window and says, 'Mrs Bundell?'

A thousand things run through my mind.

- DB has done a runner without paying.

- He's left that ruddy bag behind AGAIN.

- His dodgy knees have completely given up the ghost after yesterday's route march.

But no. This is another taxi driver. The correct taxi driver. The taxi driver who is running us to the airport. So, whose cab am I sitting in? The wrong taxi driver. The taxi driver, who's waiting to take someone else somewhere else— probably to the rubbery saw mines.

I follow the right taxi driver to the right cab to find DB waiting in the back seat.

'Where have you been?' he asks churlishly. 'I've been waiting ages!'

'No, *I've* been waiting ages,' I reply equally churlishly.

Pause.

'Just in the wrong cab,' I add meekly.

I get in beside DB and wonder if, this time, things will go smoothly. I look for the positives:

1. This isn't the same taxi driver that took us to our hotel at the beginning of the holiday.

2. He can't take us to the wrong airport – Krakow only has one.

3. He isn't Chinese.

THE BEST SEAT IN THE HOUSE

The New Forest is our latest port of call for a short break, so we start the day with a beautiful walk, breathing in the fresh air and enjoying the beauty around us.

Of course, with the aforementioned fresh air, it's not long before DB's gastric juices are luring him to the nearest tearoom for some sustenance. It's lunchtime by now, and the tearoom is heaving with people, so we're not holding out much hope of getting a table, but the waitress tells us there is, in fact, one table free and shows us, rather sheepishly it has to be said, to a small table at the back of the tearoom.

'Funny,' I say, 'did you notice she seemed a bit apologetic about putting us here?'

'Yes, I thought that.' agrees DB. 'Looks alright to me,' he adds as he goes to sit down. It's only when he tries to squeeze his sizeable breadbasket behind the table that we understand the problem. The table is wedged into a small alcove with no space to move the chair either backwards or forwards.

The choice is simple: forego lunch or risk impalement by table edge. I take one look at DB's face. Impalement it is, then.

Settling ourselves to look at the menu, we soon realise the only solution to avoid serious damage to our vital organs is to keep breathing in as much as possible.

We're just beginning to feel a little light-headed with lack of oxygen when we notice another downside to the position of the table. It's jammed between the ladies' and gents' toilets.

Now, this would not be ideal at the best of times, but when you're in a caff populated by pensioners with an average age of 80. And they're all drinking tea for England. And it's cold weather. You can see why the WCs are in overdrive.

The route past our table is like a geriatric Brands Hatch. No sooner has someone come out of the loo than another one zooms in, in a strong waft of Deep Heat.

This would be annoying enough, but the toilet hand dryers are obviously fixed to the other side of the flimsy partition wall next to us, so every time someone dries their hands, our table vibrates violently.

Picture the scene…we're not only blue-lipped with lack of oxygen, and choked by embrocation, but we're also trying to quell the vibrating table as we watch the tea slop over the top of our cups and our sausage rolls bounce their way towards the table edge like over-eager lemmings.

Worse still, when both ladies' and gents' hand dryers are used simultaneously, not only does the table shake, but we do, too. It feels like we've been tethered to one of those vibrating weight loss machines on turbo charge.

'N-n-never m-m-mind,' I pulsate as I trap a peripatetic plate with my hand. 'W-w-we'll be two s-s-stone l-l-lighter by the end of l-l-lunch.'

I look at DB, who is bouncing up and down like an elderly Duracell bunny. We both decide enough is enough and make our way, still vibrating with every step, to the exit.

Who knew a sleepy tearoom in the middle of the New Forest could be so perilous?

THE DRINKS ARE ON US!

We're in Broadstairs for a couple of nights to celebrate my Dearly Beloved's birthday. As a treat, I book a seven-course tasting menu at the hotel. However, it soon occurs to us that the last time we tried one of these multi-course tasting menus, we were young and didn't have to worry about the problems of digestion that come with *'a certain age.'* Now, half a century on, we look at the menu, created with skill and loving care by a top-class chef, and realise it is fraught with danger.

There's Salt baked beetroot—perilous with blood pressure.

There's Kale—ditto with warfarin.

There's Beef—ditto with a dodgy heart.

There's Chocolate soufflé—ditto with migraine.

There's Cheese—just ditto.

The question is, will we survive as far as the coffee, or will a postprandial trip to A and E be on the cards? Reassured by the fact that upstairs, we're armed with an extra-large bottle of Gaviscon, we decide to give it our best shot.

But there's another factor to this meal that would terrify any self-respecting cardiologist. Each course comes with a different glass of wine. Now, I'm no Albert Einstein, but that's seven glasses of wine by my reckoning. Seven glasses of wine in anyone's book—is a LOT!

'I don't think we should have every glass of wine,' I say cautiously.

'Totally agree,' DB concurs. 'We'll just have one or two; that'll be plenty.'

The wine waiter arrives and pours our first glass....and our second.... and, despite our best intentions, our third. The fourth is offered. I put my hand over my glass.

'No more for me, thank you,' I say.

'Oh, go on then, just one more,' says DB after only a nanosecond's hesitation.

I give him a look. The kind of look that, in my teaching career, I kept for especially naughty Year Nine's.

'What?' he says somewhat indistinctly. 'They're only small glashes.'

'Well, have some more water, then,' I cajole in the hope that it might dilute the alcohol.

'Can't drink too much water at thish time of night,' DB slurs, 'Not with my proshtate.'

I sigh.

'Look into my eyes,' I say.

'Aw, that'sh romantic!'

'No, it's not; I want to see if you can still focus.'

DB looks crestfallen. He says something to me that I don't catch.

'What did you say?' I ask.

'I don't know. What DID I say?'

'I don't know. That's what I'm asking YOU!'

'Oh, right. What was I talking about?'

'Don't ask me! What WERE you talking about?'

'Don't know. Can't remember.'

That settles it, the dessert wine and port are definitely staying in the bottle, birthday or no birthday!

The meal finishes, and we both manage to haul our respective paunches upstairs to the room and collapse on the bed.

'Blimey! I'm full!' declares DB. 'I couldn't eat or drink another thing!'

Not ten minutes later, as I'm removing my makeup in the bathroom, I hear some strange clinking and crackling.

'What's that?' I shout through the door.

'Just having a cuppa and a biscuit,' replies DB. 'Never go to bed on an empty stomach is my motto.'

UN-BE-LIEVABLE.

The following day, DB wakes surprisingly bright and breezy and even manages to polish off a substantial breakfast.

'I have one last birthday treat in store for you,' I say tantalisingly. 'We're going to Morelli's. It's an authentic Italian ice cream parlour in Broadstairs that everyone raves over.'

DB's eyes light up. With DB's passion for ice cream, I couldn't have given him a better present. Well, perhaps a Ferrari. That might have topped it, but it would be a close-run thing.

The weather is lovely, so after breakfast, we set off for a walk along the esplanade.

'Is this the way to Morelli's?' DB asks, trying to sound casual.

'No, it's in the opposite direction,' I tell him.

'Oh. Just thought we were going to Morelli's today,' he says wistfully.

'We are, just not at 9.30 in the morning after an enormous breakfast.'

'Really? Is it that late!'

I know what's happening. Once the mention of ice cream has been made, he's like a dog with a bone. A big bone. Like a Brontosaurus Rex-sized bone.

'Let's walk for a while; we can find Morelli's later.'

By this, I mean sometime in the afternoon 'later', but DB, the ice cream junkie, is thinking more like five minutes 'later'.

We carry on walking, with DB dragging his heels like a sulky kid and throwing longing looks over his shoulder every few seconds towards the vicinity of the ice cream parlour.

We eventually loop back towards the town. DB is like a new man. There's a distinct skip in his step, and his eyes shine in anticipation of the untold delights of banana splits, knickerbocker glories, and chocolate nut sundaes.

It's only late morning, and we have all day at our disposal, so I say, 'Let's have a look around town. There's supposed to be some lovely Art shops here.'

'Art shops? ART shops?' he splutters in outrage, 'what about an ICE CREAM shop!'

'Not now; it's far too near lunchtime for an ice cream,' I reply, much to his utter horror as he faces the prospect of having to go cold turkey for another couple of hours.

Later, I spot a cafe that overlooks the sea, and we order a sandwich. 'This is a nice place for a leisurely lunch,' I say. It's the word 'leisurely' that tips DB over the edge.

'Stuff "leisurely"!' is his reply, by now a broken man. 'Get that sandwich down your neck pronto because I'm off to Morelli's, like it or not!'

Realising I'm fighting a losing battle, I do as I'm told and, fighting off dyspepsia, follow in DB's wake as he strides towards the ice cream parlour like a man possessed.

We sit down in the retro surroundings while DB marvels at the menu, which offers every known combination of ice cream confection you can imagine—and quite a few you can't.

I choose a simple Coke float while he goes for the full monty and orders the Black Forest sundae: a concoction consisting of three different flavours of ice cream, black cherry puree, two swirls of double cream, and just to guarantee an ensuing diabetic coma, chocolate sauce! It's accompanied by two spoons.

'Why two spoons?' asks DB suspiciously.

'Most people share,' replies the waiter.

DB looks at him as if he's a lunatic, and I choke on my Coke float. Hell could freeze over before that happens!

DB begins to demolish the ice cream mountain before him, all the time warily eyeing me and the spare spoon just in case I should be tempted.

It doesn't take long before there is much noisy scraping of the last dregs from the glass dish. DB is a very happy birthday boy. My job is done.

THE PRIMAEVAL SWAMP

We are away for a few days in pretty Bosham near Chichester. The weather is glorious, so DB suggests an idyllic walk along the road, which runs by the water's edge. Now, those of you who have read so far will be screaming, 'Noooo! Don't do it!' at this point.

Mindful of DB's previous 'idyllic' walks when we have variously sampled the delights of a building site, a housing estate, or an abandoned industrial zone, I ply him with questions.

'We're not going to get lost this time, are we?'

'No!'

'Is it far?'

'No.'

'Will I need proper walking shoes?

'No.'

'Are we likely to…'

'NO! Now, can we get on with it before it gets dark!'

Against my better judgement, and only after DB waves a street map, which the receptionist has given him, do I agree to go along.

All starts well, but that is no guarantee that all will finish well!

We come to the end of a paved road and reach a large area of shingle. Not a water's edge in sight.

'Hmmm!' says DB, scratching his head. He turns the map this way. Then that way. Then, this way again before more head-scratching ensues.

'We're not walking across shingle, are we!' I say suspiciously. 'I'm wearing a pair of brand-new white shoes.'

'It's fine, we pick up the road again just round that bend,' he insists and lopes off. I scamper along behind as if walking on hot coals in a desperate attempt to save my new shoes from being annihilated by sharp stones.

We follow the bend round, and surprise, surprise, there's no road to be seen. Instead, we are faced with an expanse of wet, green, slimy seaweed with the sea hundreds of metres in the distance.

'And did you happen to check the time of low tide, by any chance?' I ask with just a tinge of sarcasm.

'Maybe. Maybe not,' prevaricates DB. 'Come on, we can't turn back now; just keep going.'

I begin wading through a sea of slippery green gloop, which wouldn't look out of place on the set of 'Alien.' DB, meanwhile, strides on ahead in his sturdy trainers, oblivious to the fact that I'm in danger of going a purler with every step.

'This slimy stuff is disgusting,' I complain, but DB isn't feeling sympathetic.

'It's marine algae,' he corrects, 'thinking it's slime is all in the mind.'

'Well, my neural receptors are telling me that this stuff has definitely reached fully fledged slime-hood!' I protest as another panic-stricken slither almost deposits me on my backside in a pool of particularly nasty primaeval ooze.

By now, my brand-new white shoes are a fetching shade of lime green, and I've jiggered my back thanks to the effort of keeping upright. To add insult to injury, a small crowd has gathered on the harbour wall to watch this pair of old crocks (which, ironically, in footwear terms, is just what I need) pick their way over the treacherously slippery rocks. I imagine the comments:

'Have they been shipwrecked?'

'Must be a pair of illegal immigrants.'

'The geriatric ramblers club has got the map upside down again.'

'Ooh, look at that ghastly pair of green shoes.'

Eventually, we reach a slipway, which DB heaves me up onto. Now, on 'terra firma,' I feel a swift kick up DB's backside with one of my green shoes might be satisfying, but I reckon the onlookers have had enough entertainment for one day.

However, what's the saying? 'Hell hath no fury like a woman whose brand-new white shoes are ruined.'

Revenge shall be mine—eventually.

TRAVELS WITH TINTIN

My birthday celebration this year is a short break in Bruges, Belgium—home of Tintin, the intrepid young red-haired adventurer of cartoon fame who happens to be the double of my Dearly Beloved. Well, the hair is, not the young bit, nor the intrepid bit, not even the adventurer bit actually, but otherwise, a dead ringer.

Now, another birthday for any woman my age is never a thrilling prospect. However, something happens tonight that momentarily gives me a glimmer of hope. Well, sort of. Let me explain.

As we head out to find a restaurant for dinner, we see a small supermarket and decide to stock up on water. DB offers to take it back to the hotel while I wait in the street where most of the restaurants are located. Thinking he wouldn't be a mo', I wander up and down the street looking at the menus. Time passes, and still, DB hasn't appeared. I've examined all the menus by now, so I'm left hanging about on my own like some ageing floozie outside one particularly lively restaurant.

'Ah, madam,' says a young, good-looking waiter touting for business, 'You want to eat something?'

'Not yet, thank you. I'm waiting for my husband,' I explain.

The waiter looks at me and smiles. 'No, a lovely lady like you—you no need your husband. I introduce you to my friend. He very nice. He will give you dinner.'

'No, no, really,' I protest, but secretly rather flattered, picturing someone tall, dark and handsome.

'He got lots of money,' the young waiter continues.

'Has he?' I say, thinking, 'Result! A drop-dead gorgeous man wants to give me dinner, AND he's loaded!'

'Yes,' he continues, 'he owns this restaurant.' And he gives a sort of Belgian nudge, nudge, wink, wink.

'Really?' I simper. 'He owns the restaurant? And so young? How wonderful!'

I'm just practising my best, alluring look when he points to the doorway. 'See. There is my friend there. I introduce you.'

I look to where he's pointing but can't see his good-looking friend anywhere—just an old guy who's somewhat follicle-y challenged, with a bit of a beer belly.

Then the truth dawns. The old guy IS the 'friend'. My bubble is well and truly burst!

Just then, DB arrives. I grab his arm and hurry him along the street.

'What's the rush?' he asks.

'Well, I've just been propositioned by that young waiter,' I say a tad smugly.

'What, the one with the guide dog?' DB says, cracking up at his own joke.

I give him a murderous look and look for a restaurant that can give us two separate tables.

***

So, the highlights of today start at breakfast. We wait to be shown to a table. The waitress is from the Netherlands and has a strong accent, characterised by pronouncing words starting with 's' as 'sh'. We are perfectly in control of ourselves until she tells us, 'You can sit at this table—or you can sit over there—in fact, you can sit anywhere.' Cue much stifled childish giggling on our part!

After breakfast, we go for a walk, which proves trickier than you'd think. Bruges has cobbled streets and pavements with no distinguishing demarcation. This means that unless you have hearing that rivals a bat, you're in danger of being mown down by marauding cyclists every five minutes. And furious tringing of cycle bells tell me that somehow, that's all my fault! Now, I can't speak a word of Flemish, probably just as well, but I realise that 'go forth and multiply' in sign language is the same all over!

It's soon lunchtime. 'Let's try something local to eat,' suggests DB. I look at the menu but try as I might, I can't get my head around something called 'Flemish stew'. Yes, I know it's 'flemish' and not 'phlegmish ' but still... So, I go for that other Belgian delicacy—waffles and ice cream. Much tastier in my book.

Fortified by a double whammy of calories, we set off again in the rain. Now, normally, this wouldn't pose a problem—get the trusty brolly out, and you're good to go. But in this holiday hotspot, if you dare raise an umbrella above shoulder level, you've got forty Korean tourists following you before you can say Kim Jong Un!

Tonight, we decide to try a recommended restaurant, which had been full last night. It's a bit of a schlep, especially in the driving rain, but we know it'll be worth it when we get there.

Wrong. It's shut.

Perhaps we're too early, I think.

'It says GESLOTEN OP WOENSDAGEN, on the door. What the heck does that mean?' I ask DB.

He shrugs his shoulders. 'No idea. Opening soon? Back in ten minutes?'

A local, sensing our dilemma, translates for us…Closed on Wednesday.

Well, of course! Any fool knows that a highly recommended restaurant in the middle of a tourist hot spot closes on a Wednesday. Maybe that nice waiter from last night can fix me up with his friend after all.

***

The following day is my actual birthday. How would I sum it up? One word. Hazardous.

It starts well. It's a lovely morning; windy, but the sun is shining, and all's right with the world. Well, apart from being another year older (better make that 22 now!). Then it starts.

Hazard number one.

We're in the marketplace. Mindful of those *^#?!*@# cobbles that trip you up at every opportunity, DB, somewhat hampered by the size of his plates of meat, keeps his eyes downcast....and walks straight into the huge wing mirror of a parked truck, cracking the side of his head with a resounding clunk. Now, with DB's medical history, that's definitely not the best thing that could happen, so I mentally prepare myself for yet another trip to A and E, wondering how the heck I'm going to explain his complicated medical record in Flemish when the only phrase I know is, 'Closed on Wednesday!'

I wait for him to crumple to the ground in agony and then damn near strangle him when he merely rubs his head and says, 'Ouch, that hurt.' Meanwhile, my adrenaline levels have shot through the roof, and I need a lie-down.

165

Hazard number two.

A canal cruise is next on the list, so we join the end of a very long queue.

'Great, we're going to be stuck at the back.' I grumble to DB. 'Fat chance of getting any decent pictures when they'll all have the back of someone's head in them.'

The boat arrives, and surprisingly, everyone rushes towards the stern. Now, I should have been suspicious. Why did they do that? And why is the driver wearing a waterproof jacket when the sun is streaming down? This is a case for Tintin to solve, but my Tintin is too busy bagging the vacant seat at the front before anyone else gets it.

'Ah, life on the ocean wave,' I think as I close my eyes and feel the wind in my hair. I'm just picturing myself on the prow of 'Titanic' a-la-Kate Winslet when the wash of another boat crosses our bows, and I'm smacked in the mush by a bucketload of canal water. Gasping with shock, my fantasy is brought to an abrupt and soggy end. Tintin, who is sitting behind me is amused no end by this and remains as dry as a bone. Sod.

Hazard number three.

Did I mention it is windy? Think typhoon. We're sitting in a pavement cafe for lunch when a huge gust of wind whirls around the square. Paper napkins and menus fly in all directions, and I just manage to anchor my half-eaten panini to the plate before it scarpers, too. Suddenly, there's a loud crash, and I look on in horror as an enormous parasol in the next cafe becomes airborne and cartwheels towards us. Great, I think we've narrowly managed to avoid decapitation and death by drowning, only to be impaled on the spokes of a giant umbrella. This city is more dangerous than Beirut! Thankfully, it veers off course at the last minute and misses us by a couple of feet.

So, it's safe to say that this birthday has been pretty high-octane. It's not good for a woman of my age. That's 22, remember?

***

So, we're homeward bound, but not before we live through another real-life Adventure with Tintin.

DB has always been partial to a bit of postcard writing. He's been firing them off all week, and the hotel has been kind enough to post them for him.

This morning, he has one last card to post but forgets to give it to the receptionist, so we're on a quest to find a post box. We've been walking for quite some time but there's still no pesky post box to be seen. Never known for his patience, DB has taken to muttering to himself.

'Never find a post box when you need one'... 'Don't they post things in Belgium? We'll be home before the ruddy postcard arrives.'

'I bet Postman Pat doesn't have this problem, eh?' I quip, trying to lighten the mood.

Nothing.

'Don't worry,' I try again. 'It won't matter if you don't send it.'

DB looks at me as if I've suggested he's a serial killer.

We turn a corner, and hallelujah! We spot an official-looking post box on a wall, much to DB's delight.

He pops the postcard into the box and triumphantly dusts off his hands. Job done.

We walk a few hundred metres further on and....oh dear... there in front of us is an even MORE official-looking post box. I mean REALLY official, with a huge P for Post on it.

'Er, what's this?' I say with a feeling of impending doom.

DB looks at the post box, then back along the street to the post box he used.

The truth dawns.

DB has posted his card in someone's private post box.

We run back to the box to see if he can retrieve the card somehow.

'You keep a lookout; I'll see if I can fish it out,' he says. There's a strange glint in his eye and I have a suspicion that he's relishing the adventure. Suddenly, he's in the imaginary realm of Tintin for real.

The actual Tintin would crack a problem like this in a few minutes, I think. But then the actual Tintin wouldn't have been so stupid as to post a card in the wrong box in the first place!

He peers into the narrow slot first with one eye, then with the other—as if that will make any difference! Then he tries sliding his fingers in to see if he can lever it out, but to no avail.

'Stop it. We're going to be arrested,' I hiss, uncomfortable with my assumed role of gangster's moll. 'Isn't interfering with the Queen's mail a criminal offence?'

'That's in England,' he tells me, tongue out in concentration.

'Well, doesn't it mean any Queen? Hasn't Belgium got a Queen? I'm sure Belgium has a Queen.' I prattle on nervously.

Eventually, after a few more tries, he has to admit defeat, and we leg it before the Belgian constabulary catches up with us.

Our only consolation is the house owners will probably never know who put a card in their post box, let alone understand that the cryptic message, 'Weather dreadful. Wish you were here!' is just a typical British attempt at humour.

TRIP TO THE LOO, MY DARLIN'

We're treating ourselves to a weekend away in Suffolk. We arrive at the hotel, which is an old coaching Inn where both Dickens and Thackeray stayed, and while the rooms have been refurbed to the highest spec, the same can't be said for the ancient corridors, which slope not only downwards but sideways too. We soon discover that the only way to avoid looking like a pair of winos who have just staggered in from the nearest boozer is to lean at a 45-degree angle and keep our eyes fixed on the horizon.

Slightly queasy, we eventually arrive at our room—also blessed with a crazily undulating floor—and start to unpack. I go to put my toilet bag in the bathroom, which is down a couple of steep stairs, and discover that the sloping floor, along with the sudden downward trajectory from the precipitous steps, catapults you into the loo with a kind of frenzied canter. I'm just making a mental note never to drop the toilet roll when I spot another more serious hazard.

This bathroom has the lowest toilet pan in the world! Seriously, it's barely a foot off the floor. Put it this way: if a toilet had featured in Snow White and the Seven Dwarfs, it would have towered over this one.

'Have a look at this,' I call to DB.

'Do I have to?' he complains, 'I'm just getting my sea legs after navigating those dreadful corridors.'

'That'll pale into insignificance when you see this,' I say.

DB, also caught out by the steps, hurtles into the loo, stops in astonishment, and exclaims, 'What the….'

'Told you,' I say.

'How am I supposed to get down there?' he asks. 'More importantly, with my dodgy knees, how am I supposed to get back up!'

I assess the situation, but no matter how you look at it, having to haul yourself up from virtually ground level is not only going to need two knee replacements but is likely to induce a nasty bout of the bends. I briefly wonder a) if there's a Beck and Pollitzer crane hire handy. b) will we be stuck in the toilet for the rest of the trip? And c) is it humanly possible to hold onto 48 hours' worth of wee without resulting in a trip to Casualty?

None of them sounds a cert, so it's a case of fingers (or should that be legs) crossed and hope for the best.

'Well, there's one thing for sure,' I say to DB. 'I'll be giving the complimentary bottles of water a miss! Dehydration is the name of the game for the next two days.'

That night, as we settle down to sleep, it dawns on us that because the floor in our bedroom slopes backwards, the bed does too. By two in the morning, we wake up with our heads rammed into the headboard and necks like Quasimodo! DB decides a trip to the loo is necessary if only to straighten out his neck and sallies forth, forgetting that the bathroom floor slopes alarmingly downhill. Never fully compos mentis at the best of times, DB, still half asleep, takes an unexpected swerve past the toilet and careers headlong into the edge of the bath. By morning, he can add two bruised knees plus neck damage, to the souvenirs of our stay.

Tonight, however, crowns it all. I foolishly wear some high heels to dinner (not JUST high heels. That would be weird). Coming into the restaurant, I hit a dodgy floorboard, and that, combined with the heels, makes me execute a kind of Dick Emery 'Ooh, you are awful, but I like you' stagger (for those of you who are old enough to remember who Dick Emery is!). This propels me towards an unsuspecting diner who is just lifting a spoonful of soup to his mouth. I nudge his elbow as I stagger to regain my balance, knocking the spoon sideways, slopping soup down his shirt! Aargh!

I give him my profuse apologies and wonder for an instant if I should offer to mop him down with his napkin. Dearly Beloved, sensing what is going through my mind, gives me a look that would make a gorgon proud and drags me away before I can wreak any more havoc.

So, if you ever feel the urge to stay in a historic pile, bring a supply of sea sickness tablets, a neck brace, and flat shoes!

UP THE RHINE WITHOUT A PADDLE

The Bundells have gone AWOL again—this time on a river cruise down the Rhine.

Had we but world enough and time, I'd recount the whole sorry saga of our journey to Basel, where we were due to pick up the ship. Suffice it to say, if you read about the travails of our previous trips and thought they were bad, this journey was EVEN MORE FRAUGHT in HUGE capital letters!

The short version goes like this…

Plane is cancelled less than 12 hours before we're due to leave. No reply from BA, no reply from Cruise Line, no reply from Travel Insurance Co. Left in limbo screaming impotently down the phone at various disembodied voices which promise us, 'Your custom is really important to us,' but clearly not important enough to pick up the flaming phone!

A mounting sense of panic sets in that we will miss the boat, both literally and metaphorically.

Four frantic hours later, the travel agent gets back to us, probably terrified that the madwoman who has left the plethora of vitriolic answer phone messages is in danger of complete meltdown.

The alternatives she suggests unfold like a second-rate melodrama.

We've been rescheduled for a later flight– HURRAH!—which will get into Basel AFTER the departure time for the boat to leave—BOO!

Another phone call assures us that the Captain will wait—HURRAH! But only for a few hours—BOO!

We ring the taxi company which is due to take us to the airport to find that the slots for the day are full, so we either have to travel to the airport at the original time or hitchhike down the M25, trundling our cases behind us. We decide a 7-hour wait in the peace and tranquillity (note heavy sarcasm) of Airport Departures is marginally preferable.

We sally forth at the crack of dawn and wait the interminable 7 hours only to be told that now our rescheduled flight is delayed by 2 hours. We go in search of any BA official to garrotte, but they all seem to have conveniently scarpered.

After 9 hours of incarceration in the hell hole that is Heathrow, we console ourselves that if ever faced with a life sentence in Belmarsh prison, it'll be a walk in the park.

We eventually get on the plane, but, of course, we've now missed our take-off slot—along with many others by the look of the line of jets queuing nose to tail on the tarmac like an aeronautical rush hour.

At last, we hear the words we've been waiting for,

'Clear for take-off.'

Halle-bloomin'-lujah! But it wouldn't be a true Bundell saga if that was the end of it. Oh, no, not by a long chalk….

At last, we get clearance from air traffic and take off. 'About flaming time!' says DB, whose stress levels reached stratospheric some hours ago.

Then comes a message over the tannoy, which just about finishes him off.

'Due to our late take-off, we have a limited selection of food and drink on board.'

'What?' splutters DB. 'They're telling me that after all those hours of waiting, all I'm going to be offered is a measly sandwich!'

However, a measly sandwich, it turns out, would have been a luxury.

Instead, the cabin crew, rather sheepishly, begin dishing out packets of crisps and miniature bottles of water.

And that's it. Nothing else. Nada. Zilch. Zero.

I manage to placate DB with the fact that we're all in the same boat (or should that be plane?) when the business class steward walks down the aisle with an enormous plate of goodies, which he's unsuccessfully tried to conceal with a linen napkin.

That does it. DB is apoplectic.

'You're kidding me!' he protests, which becomes the forerunner to a rant about the prevailing inequalities of the class system.

'Yes, dear,' I say as I munch my crisps.

We arrive at Basel looking forward to relaxing with a nice glass of wine and something substantial to eat after our diet of crisps and water, but immigration has different ideas. We're faced with a long queue, and I mean first day of the January sales long, peppered with screaming kids and irate Italians.

It takes another 2 hours to get through immigration before we emerge from the terminal, slap bang in the middle of a thunderstorm, which necessitates us driving to the boat at a snail's pace.

DB's digestive system has seen off the plane's paltry packet of crisps long ago, so he is positively drooling at the thought of something decent to eat, but alas, it is not to be. The kitchen on board closed hours ago, and we've been left with a couple of fancy but inadequate rolls in our cabin and, you've guessed it, a bottle of water!

DB is thunderous. The end of a diabolical day, you might say. But not quite…

Exhausted and looking forward to hitting the sack, we quickly unpack and change into our PJs before scoffing our sarnies. I pick up the litre bottle of water to open it and inexplicably, the glass bottom falls clean out of it! A tsunami of cold water cascades everywhere. It's like a scene from The Titanic—except DB is no Leonardo DiCaprio!

Anyway, my PJs are soaked, the carpet is soaked, and the clothes that had still to get as far as the wardrobe are soaked.

It was literally a case of, 'Water, water everywhere nor any drop to drink.'

'Brilliant!' exclaims DB who is now not only ravenous but parched to boot.

His good humour is soon restored, however, when he looks at my saturated state and finds it positively hilarious when I tell him this is the one and only pair of pyjamas I've brought with me!

In revenge, I point out that as he's the one who's bone dry, he's also the one who has to get dressed again to get more towels and explain that within 30 minutes of arrival, we've managed to flood one of their impeccable cabins.

Meanwhile, I squelch across the carpet, grab the hairdryer and start blasting myself with hot air in the vain hope of drying out my soggy pyjamas. Sensing I look like I'm trying out a new type of flagellation for wimps, I pray the captain doesn't burst in with an order to walk the plank for ruining one of his best cabins.

DB returns with the steward, who tries his best to avert his eyes from the stomach-churning sight of a clapped-out old biddy attired in sodden nightwear and mops up as much

177

as he can. He quite sensibly draws the line at also mopping up said old biddy, who reconciles herself to the fact she's going to be sleeping in her underwear!

The day from Hell is over at last.

VIVA ESPANA!

So, DB and I are seeking some sun in Spain. We have to leave at silly o'clock, so we forgo breakfast. Now, anyone who knows DB knows nothing comes between him and his stomach, so he's feeling slightly miffed.

'I'll have to take some bananas, or I'll be starving!' he declares.

I point out that airports do sell food, but this doesn't quell his fears that malnutrition is imminent.

We get everything in the car, but just as we're about to set off, DB yells, 'Wait! I've forgotten the bananas.'

Handbrake on, engine off and he disappears back into the house.

Some minutes later, he reappears with a jacket.

'Thought I'd bring this just in case it's chilly.'

We're about to set off again when, 'Wait! I've forgotten the bananas.'

Handbrake on, engine off, and he disappears into the house again.

I'm suffering a strong sense of déjà vu when five minutes later, he's back. This time with the bananas.

'Here, can you put them somewhere?' he asks.

I imagine a lot of places I'd like to put them. None of them are polite.

'I don't want them,' I say tetchily.

'Ok, Ok, I'll put them in the boot.'

'Stop right there,' I say as he reaches for the handbrake. 'Just put them on the back seat, or we'll never get there!'

We get to the airport car park, drag our cases out, and get settled on the shuttle bus.

'Wait! I've left the bananas on the back seat of the car!'

By this time, 'bananas' is a precise description of my mental state.

DB leaps off the bus and rescues his ruddy bananas. To avoid any more stress, I wedge them into the minuscule space left in my bag, and we set off for the terminal.

We check in, sit down, and wait for our flight to be called.

'I'll have one of those bananas now,' DB says, licking his lips in anticipation.

I dive into my bulging bag and bring out two squished, slimy brown bananas. DB looks at them in silent disgust.

'I can't eat those, they're disgusting!'

I now have two choices: ram them down his throat, preferably sideways, or get rid of them.

It's tempting.

Very tempting.

But good wife that I am, I find the nearest bin.

***

We've settled into the hotel and spent the last couple of days by the pool. But as it's a bit breezy today, we decide to explore a little further and take the bus to a market in a pretty nearby port. Now, if it's breezy at the hotel, it's positively gale force here!

Undaunted, I drag DB around the stalls. Who knew a market could be such a hazard on a breezy day! Everything that's hanging from the stalls is being tossed about in the wind, so it doesn't take long before DB's thoroughly cheesed off by being smothered by whirling dresses and slapped on the back of the head by flapping T-shirts. It's being smacked in the mush by an oversized bra that finally does it.

'Right, that's it!' he declares. 'I'm going for a drink!'

We head towards the marina, which I point out is going to be the windiest place in an already windy place, but traumatised by his close encounter with ladies' underwear, he sits down in the harbour-side cafe anyway.

It's me who draws the short straw, natch, and sits with the full force of the wind in my face. I'm beginning to look as if I've had one of those dodgy Hollywood facelifts when the waitress takes our order. DB can't decide between a beer or an ice cream, so he has both (yeh, not a combination that

181

would be high on Marcus Wareing's list of recommendations). Just as he lifts the first spoonful of ice cream to his lips, it becomes airborne and splatters down the front of his new tee shirt.

'Look at that! Bloomin' wind!' he complains, rubbing at the stain. The words are hardly out of his mouth when another gust tips his beer glass over, and I watch, horrified, as an amber river of beer heads, as if in slow motion, inexorably towards my lap.

'Nooooo!' I jump up, but too late, I'm soaked.

'Look at what your beer's done!' I growl, but DB's too intent on rubbing at his minuscule ice cream stain.

'Look at that! My tee shirt is in a right mess!' is his only reply.

Now, I don't know about you but faced with the choice of a small ice cream blob on my tee shirt or a pair of beer-soaked white trousers, I know which one I'd choose. Just saying.

I try to mitigate as much of the damage as possible by blotting the yellow stain with some napkins, but no matter how I try, I still look as if I'm losing the battle with a serious incontinence problem. We head for the bus to take us back to our hotel with me walking like John Wayne and DB rubbing furiously at his stomach every few minutes. It's no surprise, I suppose, that we have no problem getting two seats to ourselves!

***

So, I'm at the pool while DB, whose clothes mysteriously seem to have shrunk by several sizes, is trying to work off a week's overindulgence. My parasol won't stay up, and the sun-kissed look I'm aiming for is rapidly becoming more overdone pork chop.

In desperation, I give the parasol one more go.

And that's when I trigger a series of disasters. To reach the catch easier, I stand on the edge of the sunbed. Bad decision. This tips forward; I grab the pole to steady myself and find myself careering dangerously towards the German in the next sunbed. The poor man looks up and sees what appears to be an incompetent geriatric pole dancer heading straight for him!

Fearing for his life, he offers to help. Now, if he'd been the Arnold Schwarzenegger type, all would have been well, but he's tiny, minuscule—a stature that's definitely more Frankfurter than Bratwurst.

Anyway, nothing daunted, we combine efforts and at first, seem successful.

I say, 'Danke Schoen,' and instantly, the sodding thing collapses again! Now, I don't know if you've ever been trapped inside a parasol with a pint-sized German, but it's not all it's cracked up to be.

We look at each other for a long moment, then simultaneously back out red-faced and sweating, as if we'd just finished a particularly frantic Hokey Cokey. Admitting the Anglo/ German alliance isn't going to work, the pocket-sized German shrugs and returns to his sunbed, while I decide sunbathing is overrated anyway.

***

It's a little-known fact that DB is a veritable martyr to Athletes' foot, so it's hardly surprising when within 24 hours of arriving, it's giving him gip. Now, the sensible athlete's foot sufferer would always have a ready supply of lotions and potions at hand, but not DB, so off we limp to find a chemist.

He's looked up 'athlete's foot' in the Spanish phrase book, so he's confident he'll make himself understood. Sadly, not.

Dolores, the chemist's assistant, looks at him blankly. Thus begins a mime show that would put Marcel Marceau in the shade.

DB points at his foot and then grimaces.

Nada.

He hops up and down as if on hot bricks.

Nada.

He scratches his face and then points to his feet and says, 'It's very itchy.'

'Ah,' says Dolores, the light dawning. 'You 'ave skin. It very itchy!'

'Si, si,' beams DB triumphantly.

'You come,' she says and leads him to a chair.

'What's happening?' I ask.

'She's going to have a look, obvs,' he says and bends down to take off a shoe.

'No, no! You sit!' Dolores says firmly, turning all Spanish Inquisition on him as she pushes him into the chair.

She brings over a tube of cream. 'Aloe Vera,' she says.

''Allo Dolores,' quips DB in return, but the joke is lost in translation.

'It very good for skin itches,' continues Dolores, then without warning, pushes his head back, and before you can say, 'hasta la vista,' DB is having a full-blown facial!

To say he is taken aback is an understatement—DB's flabber has never been so gasted. He sits there, totally out of his comfort zone, as rigid as a dressmaker's dummy in a deep freeze. Only his eyes, wide as saucers, swivel desperately from side to side in a silent plea for help.

Of course, I'm enjoying this immensely. 'Having fun, dear?' I ask as Dolores slaps on some more cream.

'Noff Rilly,' he mumbles, his lips clamped tight against Dolores' ministrations.

I suspect that means, 'not really,' but this is the best entertainment I've had in ages, so I nod encouragingly at Dolores and say, 'He's loving it!'

The torture is over too soon in my book, and DB scarpers sharpish out the shop door.

'What just happened?' he gasps in deep shock.

'Think yourself lucky,' I tell him. 'Women would pay good money for that.' But DB's not listening. He's now (excuse the pun) hot-footing it up the road like Speedy Gonzales. Strange. His athlete's foot doesn't seem to be bothering him now....

THE ENTENTE CORDIALE

DB et moi are off on a road trip, heading to Bordeaux for a wedding. Now, for those of you who know us well, it'll hardly be 'Quelle surprise' that from the get-go, things go awry.

We're en route to the Channel Tunnel when we discover the motorway is closed, which means a diversion. We're instructed to follow the signs with the black triangle, and everything goes swimmingly until DB, who obviously needed more practice with the shape sorter when he was a child, mistakenly ignores the triangle and follows a sign with a black circle instead.

'Wait!' I yell. 'You're going the wrong way!'

'No, I'm not,' argues DB. 'I'm following the black circle.'

'You're supposed to be following the black triangle,' I remind him.

'Triangles, circles, what difference does it make?' he answers blithely.

'Well, Euclid might have something to say about that,' I say. 'Or Pythagoras. Or Einstein. Or Potty Pearce, your maths teacher,' I continue, warming to my theme.

'All right, all right! I get the drift,' DB sulks.

By now, we're well on the way to Dover—which is a bit of a bummer as we're supposed to be going to Folkestone. Dover docks hove into view, and I contemplate blagging our way onto a ferry instead, but eventually, we see a sign for Folkestone. We screech into the terminal on two wheels just in time to board the train.

Once we're in France, things get no better. Doreen, the sat nav lady, has obviously not heard of the Entente Cordiale and wants us the heck out of France ASAP. Before we can say 'sacre bleu,' she sends us down a road that is signposted, 'Le Tunnel sous la Manche!'

'Hang on a minute!' I shout. 'We're heading back to the Channel Tunnel. We've only just come through it!'

This is turning out to be the shortest road trip on record. Ten minutes on French soil, and we're heading home again!

'You'll have to do a U-turn,' I say.

'Brilliant!' mutters DB. 'Probably breaking every French traffic law going. Probably spend the rest of my life in the blooming Bastille!'

We execute said U-turn, give Doreen a good talking to, and manage to head in the right direction for the rest of the journey. Now, I could say things can only get better, but this is the Bundells—so, peut-etre, not!

***

We arrive at the first of our hotels. Now, this is a budget break, so the hotels I've booked are not exactly the most salubrious we've ever stayed in, but if this one has 1/2 star, it's 1 star too many!

Our dingy room is painted in what the Farrow and Ball catalogue might call 'Used Tea Bag', but worse than that is 'l'odeur.' Imagine the nose-stripping slam of a family pack of cut-price air fresheners, and you'll get the gist. I can't help feeling that the only reason you'd risk choking your guests with the ghastly guff of synthetic 'tropical paradise' is because something dodgy is festering in a corner somewhere.

A thorough inspection thankfully reveals nothing untoward, so to avoid suffocation, we throw open the window and escape to the bar across the road.

This is when things turn from bad to worse. There's only one table available, which happens to be slap bang in the centre of a group of irate French who seem to have forgotten that the Gallic wars are over.

An Asterix look-a-like and his oversized mate, obviously Obelix, are arguing the toss about something. A 'well-built' lady who seems to be Asterix's missus and is sporting a pair of bulging biceps and a nice line in tattoos, squares up to the chain-smoking friend. Torrents of vituperative French are exchanged, accompanied by much dramatic Gallic gesturing.

This is fun! I think, as we peer through a cloud of Galoise smoke.

The argument continues to rage around us as DB and I try to sip our drinks with typical English sangfroid.

'I feel as if we're in a crowd scene from "Les Mis",' I say under my breath. 'They'll be piling up the tables and chairs to make a barricade next!'

'Shhh!' hisses DB. 'Don't let them know we're English or we're done for!'

DB and I are faced with a tricky decision. Stay here and risk being guillotined by a braying French mob or return to our room and be asphyxiated by the synthetic pong of 'Tropical Paradise'. We take another look at the muscles on Asterix's missus. 'Tropical Paradise' it is, then.

***

The next hotel on 'Bundell's Budget Break' would give Fawlty Towers a run for its money. The room is what the French would term 'bijou', but anybody else would call Lilliputian. We open the door to the wardrobe to find it's actually the en-suite, complete with shower at one end, toilet at the other, and in the middle, for some inexplicable reason, a sink the size of a bath!

Now, DB's appreciation of the French cuisine means that his stomach is now so substantial that it needs its own postcode, so squeezing round this sink to negotiate the toilet, needs carefully planning. It requires taking a deep breath in, then a rapid sideways shuffle before the need to breathe out again risks serious internal injuries.

The Fawlty Towers comparison continues at breakfast the next day. Fresh orange juice is on offer, which necessitates pressing half an orange on an electric squeezer thingy, switching it on, and hey presto—the orange is squeezed for you.

Now, as many of you know, dexterity is not my strongest point, so it's par for the course that as soon as I touch the machine, it goes into overdrive. Panicking, I let go of the orange, which, now a free agent, whizzes across the room like a mini frisbee, almost taking the eye out of a startled guest.

The tall, skinny proprietor, or Bordeaux's Basil Fawlty as I've come to know him, watches me with horror as I simultaneously wreck his equipment and blind his guests. As he scurries over, muttering, 'Mon Dieu! Mon Dieu!' under his breath, the people at nearby tables seeing me reach for another orange, duck to take cover. Before more mayhem ensues, Basil snatches the orange out of my hand and does it for me.

Then comes the cereal fiasco. The muesli is in a dispenser with a tap at the bottom that you turn to release a small serving into your bowl. Simple enough, you'd think. But not for this ham-fisted chump. I twist it. Nothing. I twist it again.

191

Nothing. I jiggle it a bit, and WHOOSH, the entire contents of the dispenser cascade into a huge muesli mountain on the countertop.

I look around sheepishly, hoping no one's noticed, but old 'eagle eyes' has seen it all. 'Merdre! Zut alors!' and various other French expletives fill the air as he tries to repair the damage I've caused. I give up and settle for a croissant. I'm about to reach for one when he says with desperation in his voice, 'Non! I will bring you ze croissant. Please—assey-vous!'

Feeling like a naughty schoolgirl, I do as I'm told, and Basil, obviously struggling with his 'joie de vivre' ungraciously slaps a croissant on my plate before rushing off to increase his public liability insurance.

DB, who has sat through all this blithely, tucking into his own well-behaved breakfast, leaves me to it and returns to the room to squeeze his corporation around the sink again.

LOCK DOWN
LAUGHS

A BOG-STANDARD JOB

We've now completed 100 days in lockdown, and we haven't instigated divorce proceedings!

How do we celebrate?

'Let's decorate the downstairs bathroom,' I suggest, aware it's not the most romantic proposition DB's ever had.

'Or we could just open a bottle of fizz,' says DB hopefully.

So, we do both—not at the same time, you understand. Drinking a glass of Prosecco while sharing a paint-splattered loo seat would be distinctly odd—even for us!

The day starts well, DB designates himself as Chief Decorator (natch) while I'm appointed to the lowly position of Apprentice Brush Cleaner / Tea Boy.

DB gets stuck in. I count the tea bags.

Bored, I suggest, 'Why don't I paint the skirting board while you're doing the walls?' Surprisingly, since he knows my cack-handedness only too well, he agrees.

'What do you use to stir paint with?' I ask, looking at some murky white gloss in a half-used tin.

'An old stick, usually,' comes the reply from behind the loo door.

I look around the kitchen, but, unsurprisingly, we seem to be all out of old sticks, so I spy a screwdriver that DB has used to take off the door handle.

That'll do nicely, I think.

Moments later, DB's head appears round the toilet door, face aghast when he sees me stirring the paint.

'What are you doing! You don't stir gloss paint!' he remonstrates.

'You told me to,' I reply.

'No, I didn't!'

'Yes, you did!'

'Didn't'

(Pause, then sotto voce) 'Did.'

'And what's that you're using!' he demands.

I slowly take the paint-caked screwdriver out of the tin, knowing I'm in deep trouble.

'That's my best screwdriver!' he fumes. 'Look at it!'

He grabs it from me to clean, so I retreat into the loo smartish and start painting the skirting board.

Now, as you can imagine, the downstairs loo is not exactly the Albert Hall. It would be difficult to swing a hamster in there, let alone a cat. Still, with some careful choreography, we manage to dance around each other successfully. Then it happens. Facing in opposite directions, we both bend down to our respective paint tins at the same time, bum-butting each other forcefully. This plummets me towards the gaping jaws of the toilet pan while DB hurtles headfirst into his newly painted grey wall.

A nifty sidestep means I escape the horrors of an unexpected bog-wash, then I turn round to inspect if DB has escaped doing any damage. Sadly not. There's a huge smudge in the paint on the wall, while DB is now sporting some fetching grey highlights.

'You've got 50 shades of grey going on there, dear,' I say, trying to lighten the atmosphere.

'Not funny!' replies DB as he repairs the damage with a severe sense of humour failure. I decide, in the interests of marital harmony, to demote myself back to tea boy duties.

A little while later, I check to see how Laurence Llewellyn Bowen is getting on. He's made great progress, having finished the walls and glossed the door.

'Phew, it's warm in here,' I say, and fling open the window.

Why? Why did I do it?

Just as DB yells, 'Noooooo!' the open window causes a through draft, which lifts a sheet of newspaper off the floor and plasters it firmly against the fresh gloss paint.

Yesterday's news is now imprinted on the back of the toilet door.

'Just think,' I say to DB, desperately trying to dig myself out of another hole, 'You'll never have to take the newspaper into the loo again!'

Let's just say if a look can speak a thousand words, these ones are all unprintable!

THE UGLY DUCKLING!

Thanks to Boris binning Christmas, our visit to the family for the festivities is finito. For my Dearly Beloved, this is devastating on many fronts, but mainly because we are now suffering a serious turkey deficit.

Aghast at the thought that it might be a turkey-free Christmas, DB decides that this necessitates a trip to the plague pit called Waitrose (expensive, but you get a better class of virus there). I suggest that dusting off that tin of pilchards that's been lurking at the back of the cupboard since Lockdown No. 1 might be a better alternative than facing the hellhole of a supermarket two days before Christmas, but no, nothing gets between DB and his turkey dinner. So, Amazon, being completely out of hazmat suits, DB dons full PPE and sallies forth. I'm laid up with a bad back, which means that, against my better judgment, I let him loose on his own.

'Text me if there are any problems,' I say as I rub in another hefty dollop of Voltarol.

Half an hour later, I get a call.

'Right, I'm at the turkey counter—big problem, there are no turkey crowns.'

'How about a turkey tiara?' I riposte.

'Not funny. What should I do?'

'Well, just get a big chicken,' I suggest.

'A chicken? A CHICKEN? For CHRISTMAS! Don't be ridiculous!' he splutters. 'There IS something here that would do. It's a turkey variety pack with a breast, legs, stuffing balls, sausage meat....'

'And how much is that?' I interrupt.

'Er.... £65,' he mumbles quickly.

'£65!'

'But it feeds eight.'

'Yes, and there are two of us. You. Me. TWO!'

'And it comes with gravy,' he adds in a last-ditch attempt.

'I don't care if it comes with gold-plated cutlery. Put it back!'

'But I like turkey.'

'Now, listen to me.' I say slowly. 'Step away from the counter. You have seriously lost your marbles. Do NOT buy the turkey pack!'

'All right, ok, I get the message,' DB replies grumpily and rings off.

An hour later, he staggers through the back door, weighed down by shopping bags. He sees me looking at them suspiciously.

'Don't worry, I didn't buy the turkey pack,' he reassures me (though it looks like he has bought the rest of the supermarket as compensation). 'Look what I bought instead,' he says, 'it was the only one on the shelf!'

My heart plummets. 'The only one on the shelf' is never a good sign.

With a flourish, he pulls out a scrawny-looking duck who was probably last seen gracing Hilda Ogden's living room wall.

'What's that?' I say unenthusiastically.

'A duck,' he says.

'Have you gone completely quackers!' I exclaim. Wittily, in my opinion.

'What's wrong with it?' he says, disappointed that I'm not jumping up and down with glee at his brilliant find.

'Looks as if it needs a ducktor,' I continue with the bad duck jokes, but DB is in no mood for laughing.

'It's fine. It'll be tasty with a nice orange sauce.'

'What did you say at the checkout? Please put this on my BILL?' I continue unrelentingly. 'Perhaps if you'd got up at the QUACK of dawn, there would have been more to choose from.'

My brilliant badinage is falling on deaf ears, so I give up.

I look in the shopping bags at the horde of goodies that DB has bought. Christmas pudding, brandy butter, cranberry sauce, chocolate-covered nuts. We're only missing a partridge in a pear tree, and quite frankly, that would be far more appetising than the look of that emaciated duck.

DB begins to unload his Christmas haul while the duck and I eye each other warily. Might be dusting off that tin of pilchards after all.

A SET OF TIDY DRAWERS

There's a new pandemic called Lockdown Tidying Syndrome. Look out for the symptoms. It starts by tidying your knicker drawer, and before you can say 'Fung Sui', the entire house has been decluttered, and you've put your back out moving all the furniture.

Anyway, today I decide to clear the study of all the old bank statements that go so far back, the Old Lady of Threadneedle Street was nobbut a girl.

'We'll need to shred these,' I say to DB.

'Why?' he argues. 'Just chuck 'em in the bin.'

'We can't do that! What if someone gets our bank details?'

'Oh, wait, I forgot. Everyone's imprisoned on lockdown except the local gang of scurrilous bin scavengers,' he says a tad sarcastically.

'Look,' he continues, 'It'll take hours to put that mountain of paper through our piddly little shredder; let's burn them.'

'How?' I ask, slightly worried by the glint of a crazed arsonist in his eye.

'We'll use the chiminea,' he says. 'Simples.'

Now, for those not familiar with a chiminea, it's easy to describe: it's got a chimney-like thingamajig, with a kind of whatsit at the bottom on, er, a sort of whatchamacallit…

Well, anyway, you use it for heating the patio on chilly evenings.

The problem is that it's a lovely day; the sun's shining, windows and doors are open, and people are in their gardens. But too late; DB, like an impatient Pyro, is already in action with a bumper box of matches and an enormous pile of statements.

Our first problem is discovering that the paper is more Basildon Bond than Tesco's Budget. This stuff is tough! So, DB, in his infinite wisdom, decides a firelighter will help things along!

It does.

It helps things along so much that we've soon got a conflagration that wouldn't go amiss in 'Towering Inferno.'

The second problem is the thick black smoke which billows out of the top of the chiminea and heads straight for the garden of Mick, the next-door neighbour.

Now Mick is partial to a bit of sun, and he likes nothing better than sitting on the patio with his Daily Mail and a cuppa, so it's not long before we hear the frantic flapping of a newspaper and a rasping cough emanating from over the garden wall.

DB, oblivious to the mayhem he's causing, says sympathetically, 'Blimey, that's some cough poor old Mick's got. Hope it's not the dreaded virus!'

Inadvertently breathing in a lungful of the acrid smoke myself, I also begin coughing violently.

'Crikey! You've got it too!' he says, taking a few rapid steps backwards. 'I told you those cheap facemasks were useless!'

'Just get on with it,' I splutter, 'before we all choke to death!'

DB chucks the last few pages on the fire, and we go in for a much-needed glass of water.

'You smell like a kipper, old girl,' DB says in passing.

So does the conservatory, the kitchen, the dining room, the sitting room. Probably even reaches as far as my immaculately tidy knicker drawer.

THE REVENGE OF VEG

It all starts with an online shop... Now, online shopping is a complete mystery to me, but to avoid the Covid queues in supermarkets, I've given it a go, and at last, it's been delivered. Who knew that shopping could be so full of surprises! My ineptitude has meant that a large 3kg chicken actually turns out to be 3 large chickens, and what I thought would only be a week's worth of fresh veg would keep a vegan happy for a lifetime!

I look at the mound of veg and decide to blanch the excess for the freezer. After all, in this day and age, you never know where your next Brussels sprout is coming from.

Everything is going swimmingly: there are bubbling pots, pans of iced water, and blanched veg drying on tea towels in every corner of the kitchen. It's like 'Little House on the Prairie' meets 'The Waltons'. Just at that point, DB comes into the kitchen.

'Hi there, Jim Bob,' I drawl in my best American Prairies accent. 'Welcome to our mighty fine homestead.' I just stop short of shouting, 'Yee-haw!' and starting a hoedown.

DB ignores me, sniffs the air, and says, 'What is that disgusting smell! Have you been at the baked beans again?'

'No, I haven't!' I reply in righteous indignation, 'I'm blanching cauliflower! I thought you'd be pleased; you love cauliflower!'

'Cauliflower!' exclaims DB, 'Hate it!'

'Oh, well, I've done lots of broccoli, too.'

'Can't eat too much broccoli on my meds.'

'How about beans then? I've blanched tons of beans,' I say optimistically.

'Yeh, not fussed,' he says grudgingly and potters out again.

I survey the mounds of vegetables, which have taken hours to blanch, and know instantly how to exact my revenge. Once this lot is packaged and put in the freezer, there's going to be no room for DB's beloved ice cream. Shame.

AN APPLE A DAY...

We have an apple tree. It's a very nice apple tree. With very nice apples. Last year, sadly, it didn't produce much fruit, but hey, ho, that's the way the apple crumbles (boom, boom!) DB, still grieving the ensuing dearth of apple pies, decides one morning that it needs to be pruned.

Now, I'm against this on several fronts:

- DB's idea of pruning is more George Washington than Alan Titchmarsh.

- The apple tree is very tall.

- Only Spiderman could reach the top branches.

- The thought of DB in tight-fitting red and blue Lycra is putting me off my breakfast.

My reservations, unsurprisingly, fall on deaf ears, so I get the nearest A and E on speed dial and hope for the best.

The first task is to secure the ladder. Now, the apple tree variety we have is tall with a thin trunk, so there's nowhere safe for the ladder to rest.

DB pushes the ladder against the trunk. The ladder falls over. He pushes it against the trunk again. The ladder falls over. He tries a third time. The ladder miraculously stays put. Despite my doom-laden reminder that the local hospital has enough on their plate with Covid cases galore, let alone some crazy old geezer who has a blatant disregard for 'elf n' safety', he begins to climb. Unfortunately, a couple of rungs up, the ladder suddenly swivels, and he finds himself with one leg on the ladder and the other wrapped around the trunk like a semi-committed tree hugger.

'Stand on the bottom rung,' he tells me. 'Your extra weight should stabilise it.'

'Gee thanks,' I say, glad that the lockdown diet of copious cake has come in useful for something. But the grass is soft with days of rain, so now, with our combined weights, as fast as he climbs, the ladder sinks into the grass.

'What's going on!' he exclaims with his eyes fixed on the top of the tree, 'I'm getting nowhere.'

'The ground's too soft,' I explain through tears of laughter, wondering if he knows he's a dead ringer for Frank Spencer.

'Right,' says DB, 'scrap that idea. We'll have to use the work platform and the long-handled lopper.'

There are two problems with this.

1. Assembling the work platform requires a PhD in Mechanical Engineering.

2. A long-handled lopper in the hands of DB is bound to have somebody's eye out.

Anyway, nothing ventured and all that...

DB and I set forth trying to assemble said platform, but this thing has a mind of its own. As fast as one end is connected the other end collapses, so unsurprisingly, DB is soon completely hacked off with the whole thing.

Eventually, after much chuntering and scratching of the head, the platform is assembled. DB climbs onto it and then begins to wield the dreaded long-handled lopper.

Try to picture the scene: DB standing on a wobbly platform trying to control a fully extended oscillating pole so that the small clipper on the end somehow catches the top of a spindly branch that is swaying in the wind. It's like playing a game of hook-a-duck. With a ten-foot pole vault. In a tsunami. Impossible.

After a number of futile attempts, DB's tether is definitely at its end.

'This is stupid!' he thunders. 'Whose idea was this!'

'Er, yours,' I remind him. 'Look, why not try a different technique?' I suggest.

DB repositions his hands on the pole and then casts it like a fishing rod, accidentally letting go of the cord used to operate the clipper, which then wraps itself tightly around a branch far above our heads.

'Bloomin' marvellous!' he exclaims. 'Now look what you've done!'

'Me! That's rich!' I protest. 'You're the one who needs a refresher course on long-handled lopper handling.'

There follows a lot of bad-tempered pulling and yanking as he tries to disentangle the cord. At one point, so desperate is he to sort out the problem, that he ends up swinging from the end of the cord much like a decrepit Tarzan.

At last, the cord frees itself. I'm waiting for DB to beat his chest and give a Tarzan-type victory yodel, but thankfully, he spares the neighbours that delight.

Thoroughly cheesed off, Tarzan gives the whole thing up and settles for Jane making him a consolatory cuppa while the apple tree remains in its unpruned glory. Will it produce any apples this year? Probably too traumatised to ever bear fruit again!

BAH, HUMBUG!

As we Tier 3 inmates know, Christmas is different this year. Yet again, there's no chance of indulging our Christmas cheer in a tinselled Dickensian tearoom while welly-ing into a couple of mince pies; or visiting a faux Bavarian Christmas market to impulse buy a dozen boxes of hand-crafted nettle soap that will undoubtedly be 're-gifted' next year by the unlucky recipients. These are the things of Christmas Past.

I'm so lacking in Christmas spirit, I'd even welcome Mariah Carey belting out 'All I Want for Christmas' for the umpteenth time while doing a Sainsbury's shop, but Covid means we get everything online now.

So, DB and I decide to up the ante on Festive Fun and write the Christmas cards together in front of a roaring fire with some gentle carols playing in the background. (And knowing DB, mince pies will inevitably feature.)

Sounds idyllic? Well, let me warn you, this kind of 'togetherness' is best avoided if you value marital harmony.

It all starts well, with a very organised list of names and addresses in three columns: Family, Friends, and Probably-Croaked-It-But-Can't-Be-Too-Sure.

'You take column one, and I'll do column two, and we'll share column three,' suggests DB.

'An eminent idea, dear boy,' I say, getting into the Dickensian vibe as I don my imaginary fingerless gloves and chuck another lump of coal on the stove.

A pretty card picturing a plump Christmas pudding soon gets DB's gastric juices flowing.

'Time for a mince pie, I think,' he says predictably and abandons his pen for a foray into the kitchen.

Time passes.

More time passes.

I'm just beginning to think he's done a runner when DB appears, surreptitiously wiping crumbs from his mouth.

'Hurry up,' I say, 'I've written far more cards than you.'

He picks up his pen again and sets to.

I glance at the pile of cards in front of him.

'Hang on, I've written a card for Aunt Ruth in Canada.'

'No, I've written a card for Aunt Ruth in Canada.'

'I can see that,' I say. 'You're supposed to be doing column two—Friends. I'm doing column one. Family. AUNT Ruth is the clue; she's Family.'

'Oh,' he says sheepishly. 'Thought I was doing column one.'

I look at him long and hard.

'How many have you done, exactly?' I ask.

'Oh, not many,' he says quickly grabbing the pile in front of him and hiding them under the table.

'Brilliant, we've already spent the equivalent of a third-world budget on cards and stamps, and now we'll have to buy more!'

The hard-sought Festive Cheer well and truly evaporates.

'Right, it's over to you. It's my turn for a mince pie,' I say, thoroughly disgruntled with the whole card-writing exercise.

'Erm, why not have a biscuit?' says DB shiftily. 'We've got some really nice biscuits.' I ignore him. 'You like biscuits,' he shouts after me.

Entering the kitchen, I'm confronted by the relics of a packet of mince pies. DB, the human hoover, has scoffed the last two.

So, how to sum up the Spirit of Christmas at the Bundells? Let's just say the only kind of Christmas Spirit that DB will get is a crack over the head with a bottle of Baileys! Bah, humbug!

BRAIN DRAIN

I'm now blaming my senior moments on lockdown brain. Without the mental stimulation of my usual groups and activities, something has to be done to activate the old grey matter, so I decide an online quiz night might be the answer. My Dearly Beloved, however, is not of the same mind.

'Do we have to!' he moans like a sulky five-year-old.

'What's the problem?' I ask, 'You enjoy the quizzes we go to.'

'Yes, but they're fun. We're with other people, and we have a laugh. And a drink. And (finally getting to the crux of the matter) lots of nibbles.'

'Well, I'll make you a cuppa—and there's probably a stale packet of cheese and onion in the cupboard,' I add cheerily.

'Belting,' says DB, unimpressed.

The quiz starts, our pens are poised ready to write down the answers....and there they remain. These questions are so difficult that the final of 'University Challenge' looks like 'It's a Knockout' in comparison.

'This is blinkin' impossible!' DB complains as question after question leaves us both gawping at one another.

Then...

QUESTION - CAN YOU SEE THE GREAT WALL OF CHINA FROM SPACE?

'YES!' screams DB, overjoyed at finally knowing an answer.

'No,' says the quizmaster. 'It's only visible from Earth's orbit.'

'WHAT! Are you crazy?' DB screams at the screen. 'Earth's orbit IS space!'

'Well, obviously not,' I reason, 'he must mean OUTER space.'

'Look,' says DB, now with the bit between his teeth. 'Space is space. What's that bit round the Earth called? SPACE! To get to it, you've got to be in a SPACE-ship. It's SPACE!'

QUESTION - WHAT WAS GHANDI'S FIRST TWO NAMES?

'No idea,' says DB grumpily. 'Goosey, Goosey?'

Now, personally, I thought that was quite witty, but DB has completely lost his sense of humour—even for his own jokes.

QUESTION - HOW MANY BONES ARE IN A GIRAFFE'S NECK?

'You are flaming joking!' seethes DB as he throws his pen down in frustration.

He's just about to fling the laptop against the wall when the quizmaster announces that the next round is Films. Phew! DB cheers up enormously. Spending most of his youth in the 2/9's at the Odeon has come to his rescue.

QUESTION - IN WHAT FILM DID BRUCE LEE......?

But that's as far as we get because the screen starts buffering.

'No, no, don't do that!' bemoans DB, stabbing his forefinger repeatedly at the screen. 'This is the one round I'm good at!'

The screen ignores him and continues buffering... and buffering...and buffering.

'And that concludes the Film round,' declares the quiz master as the screen springs back into life again.

DB is apoplectic. It's clear that if this carries on, he's going to need another one of his pills. Pub quiz or not, I call last orders.

FLIPPIN' HORRIBLE

You know the phrase, 'I don't know whether it's Christmas, Easter, or Pancake Tuesday'? Well, that's lockdown in a nutshell. So, to me, making pancakes today when Pancake Tuesday is more than three weeks ago makes perfect sense.

I make the batter, heat some oil in the frying pan, and then cook the first pancake.

'Ooh, pancakes!' salivates my Dearly Beloved. 'Can I toss one.' he asks eagerly.

Going on past history, my mind goes into overdrive. I imagine myself at the top of a ladder, teetering precariously while scraping pancakes off the ceiling. Falling off the ladder and probably breaking a leg also feature in the mix (no pun intended!)

As queuing for hours in a coronavirus-infested Accident and Emergency is not my idea of a fun time, I decline the request. Mind you, I don't know why because if there was ever a tosser....

I serve the first pancake to myself, as it's never the best, while DB gets my second improved attempt. I add my favourite orange juice and sugar, put a forkful in my mouth, ready to savour every bit, and splutter, 'STOP! It's disgusting!'

'What?' says DB, who would eat a 'scabby dug' (as we say in Glasgow) when he's hungry. 'Mine's fine!'

Now, I don't know what flavour you like with your pancakes. Honey? Lemon juice? Maple syrup? How about curry?

You see, my Dearly Beloved cooked dinner last night, and although he quite happily follows Government guidelines and sings 'Happy Birthday' twice through while washing his hands, the same can't be said about washing the frying pan, which obviously didn't get more than the first bar of 'Humpty Dumpty'! Let's just say orange juice, sugar and CURRY pancakes is not a recipe Mary Berry will be rushing to include in her next cookbook!

Incarcerated with DB for the foreseeable, I wonder what will get me first—Coronavirus or DB's washing up!

FRECKLE FACE

I suppose the one consolation of lockdown is that it provides the opportunity to do all the jobs that you've been putting off for years.

'I'm off to paint the garden fence,' says DB.

'Oh good, I'll help,' I say as I'm beginning to go stir-crazy indoors, and it's still not lunchtime.

'No, you're all right,' answers DB with a look of horror on his face, obviously remembering the previous disaster of decorating the downstairs loo.

'Aw, let me help,' I insist, 'it'll be something to do.'

'Look. How do I put this...? You're not exactly a Picasso with a paintbrush!'

'Yeh, well, Picasso didn't paint garden fences,' I reason, 'so let me have a go.'

DB gives a deep sigh and goes to find me a paintbrush, muttering, 'This is not a wise decision, I know it.'

He returns, 'Now, before we start, you need to remember not too much on the brush, paint in one direction, and feather off the stroke so that....'

'Wait!' I stop him before he launches into a long-winded treatise on painting technique. 'Any chance we can keep this to 50 words or less, or we'll be out of lockdown before we get started!'

DB looks slightly miffed at his mansplaining being cut off in full flow but hands over the brush, and we start. We're painting some new trellis with that sticky brown preservative, so I take one side while DB takes the other.

It all starts well, but it's not long before I get a bit gung-ho about the whole thing, not to say completely narked off with the fiddly little corners of the trellis. Anyway, after one particularly hefty jab with a laden brush, I'm horrified to see an enormous spray of brown slop spurt through one of the trellis holes straight at DB.

'Oi, watch it!' he shouts, 'that got me right in the eye.' I look at his speckled face and debate whether I should tell him that's not his only problem—he has the distinct look of a cut-price Donald Trump.

I start to giggle.

'What?' he says suspiciously.

I can't speak.

'Have I got it on my face? I have, haven't I?' He scrubs furiously at his face. 'You know this stuff doesn't wash off, don't you!'

I'm still creased up.

'Do you remember that dodgy spray tan I had once? Well, this is worse! Much worse!' I say through hysterical laughter.

'Brilliant!' DB exclaims, 'I knew I couldn't trust you with a paintbrush!'

I'm obviously well and truly sacked, and as I go back into the house, I hear my phone ping. Our son, Craig, has sent a couple of photos of the grandkids. I venture into DB's man cave, aka the garage, where he's probably hibernating until the splatters wear off.

'Look at these,' I say as I show him the photos, 'Freckles obviously run in the family.'

DB is not amused.

HAPPY BIRTHDAY/ANNIVERSARY?

I have to put my hands up and admit I've forgotten our anniversary! Forty-five years ago today, I walked up the aisle to a nervously waiting DB.

It was a fabulous day, barring the fact that our best man was slightly green and swaying, having over-imbibed the night before, and that the photographer managed to capture me walking up the steps to church with the local bingo hall emblazoning 'TWICE NIGHTLY' in towering red letters behind me. That caused some raucous hilarity later! But other than that, everything was wonderful about the day.

We had had grand plans for our 45th Anniversary - dinner in a swanky restaurant, a few days away at a beauty spot, but it was not to be. With plans cancelled, I sort of expunged it from my mind as the new coronavirus routine set in, where one day was much like any other. However, my Dearly Beloved, whose mind can expunge at the drop of a hat, has put me to shame by managing a secret trip to the decimated shelves of the village shop and has bought me a card and a present.

Now, the card is not the most romantic he's ever given me, but it's the best on offer. On the front it says 'Happy Birthday' with the word 'Birthday' scribbled out and 'Anniversary' scrawled untidily above it in felt tip pen. That would have been bad enough, but it's also a child's card, so the greeting '10 today' has also been amended by my Dearly

Beloved to 'Yeh, and the rest!' But beggars can't be choosers, as they say. Nor has he exactly pushed the boat out with the anniversary present: a packet of love hearts. To share. But as the saying goes, it's the thought that counts.

So, what are our plans? Well, we might indulge in some candle-lit beans on toast followed by a quick trip to the bins and back, might even crack open a new toilet roll, but that'll be as far as the celebrations go this year.

OH DEAR, WHAT CAN THE MATTER BE…

As DB and I are now 'double injectees', we're excited about the possibility of a little more freedom, so we decide to venture out to a lovely Farm Shop in Staplehurst to indulge in some tea and scones.

We set off in the sunshine, but those pesky weather gods, spotting the Bundells on a jolly, decide to put the boot in. By the time we get there, it's blowing a gale and decidedly nippy, which, as we have to eat outside, is a bit of a pain in the proverbial, despite a large marquee having been rigged up as a shelter.

To make matters worse, we're ushered to the only free table, which Sod's law dictates, is next to the one bit of tenting in the entire marquee that has come loose and through which a veritable hooley is blowing.

'Bloomin' freezing in here,' shivers DB as he waits for his scone and tea.

'Zip your jacket up; you'll be fine,' I reply unsympathetically, the product of a Scottish upbringing where it was so cold you chipped the ice off your porridge in the mornings.

DB zips up his jacket until only his nose is showing and wraps his arms around his body for extra warmth.

Now, Covid has obviously decimated the staffing, so there's quite a wait for the tea and scones.

'I'm just going to pop into the shop for a quick breeze around,' I say.

'Breeze?' he grumbles, 'it's a force ten gale blowing through here!'

'Don't exaggerate,' I admonish, trying to stop my teeth from chattering, 'And don't start without me!'

I'm perhaps a tad longer than I intended, what with it being such a nice shop (and nothing to do with it being warm), so when I get back to the table, the tea and scones have already arrived.

'At last,' DB grumbles. 'I'm so bloomin' cold they've called the undertaker twice!'

I ignore him.

'Drink your tea,' I reply, 'that'll warm you up.'

'Ok, I'll just knock the permafrost off my hands so I can hold my teacup, shall I?'

'I haven't been that long,' I protest.

A particularly strong gust of icy wind blows through the flap of the marquee at that moment.

'Can you feel the strength of that wind?' he asks. 'My scone's blown off my plate three times waiting for you!'

He takes a sip of now tepid tea. 'And the tea's cold!'

I realise I'm in the doghouse, so we finish up quickly and go to pay at the till. But it seems the surfeit of tea, plus the cold weather, has played havoc with DB's waterworks, so he sets off to find a loo while I take the opportunity to look around the shop again.

Time passes. More time passes. Even more time passes. Still no sign of DB.

The staff in the shop are now becoming deeply wary of this shady-looking pensioner who, for the second time, is loitering by the shelves and not buying anything. It's no coincidence, therefore, that every time I turn a corner, I come face to face with the same Miss Marple, sorry, shop assistant, who eyes me suspiciously.

I try a reassuring smile, which hopefully conveys that I'm not really a shoplifter, just someone who's married to an old fogey with an obstinate prostate.

Suddenly, my phone rings. It's DB.

'What the heck are you doing?' I hiss into the speaker, 'I'm about to be arrested for shoplifting here!'

'You know the old song that starts, "Oh, dear, what can the matter be?"' he replies.

'Yes,' I say.

'Well, it's not "three old ladies that are locked in the lavatory". It's me!'

Marvellous! I now have to face Miss Marple, explain what's happened, and ask her to release DB from the toilet. She looks at me as if it's all a cunning ruse to get rid of her so I can ransack the shelves, but eventually, having put the reassuring smile into overdrive, she gives me the benefit of the doubt and releases a very red-faced DB from the Gents. She scurries back to the shelves to scrutinise them for any missing items while I frogmarch DB back to the car before we're thrown out. As we're about to set off, DB begins to look pained.

'What's the matter?' I ask.

'That whole episode took so long I might need another wee,' he says.

'Forget it! Cross your legs and don't think of running water,' I reply, as I throw the car into drive and pray there are no speed bumps on the way home!

ONE BIG KNIT!

Why on earth did I take up knitting again? It's not that I was ever any good at it! I did knit a couple of matinee jackets for my one and only when he was a baby. (By the way, *matinee* jackets? Why do babies need *matinee* jackets? How many babies do you see rocking up for an afternoon performance at the theatre? Imagine the scene in the creche:

'I say old bean, off to a matinee at the theatre this afternoon. Thought I'd wear that new matinee jacket mother knitted me.'

'Oh, rather you than me, old boy. Hate the theatre. I have a wardrobe full of matinee jackets—never worn one once.)

Anyway, I digress. My lack of knitting prowess meant that the first jacket I knitted for my newborn was somehow longer in the front than the back, which made him look like an infant Quasimodo. The second one had sleeves long enough to fit a chimp, which, when rolled up multiple times, gave him a set of biceps to rival Desperate Dan.

Either way, this mother's handiwork meant my poor babe was more likely to feature in a brochure for Dr Barnardo's than on the front cover of 'Knitting Weekly'. But in these COVID days a gal's got to keep busy, so I've set to with the knitting needles again. Banking on the hope that not even I could mangle a rectangle, I'm knitting blankets for the NICU at the local hospital.

I'm getting on swimmingly; knit one, purl one, drop one, repeat, when my Dearly Beloved comes in, looks at the work of my fair hand, and says, 'Knitting a string vest, dear? Jolly good.'

Now, take it from me, all you husbands out there; never criticise your loved one while she's holding a pair of size eight knitting needles! Particularly if, like DB, you choose that moment to bend over and pick up the newspaper from the floor.

But I restrain myself. Sacrificing an essential knitting needle just to see DB's eyes pop out of their sockets, tempting as it is, is not going to get these blankets knitted.

However, I do have another solution to his disparaging remarks – sourcing a knitting pattern for a man-sized muzzle. Just saying.

SHORT BACK AND SIDES

After weeks of lockdown, my Dearly Beloved's barnet has a touch of Worzel Gummidge about it, so the time has come for a visit to my new business enterprise—FIFI'S HAIR SALON. There's no run-of-the-mill short back and sides, buzz cuts, or quiffs here. At FIFI'S SALON, we specialise in a brand-new style—The Covid Cut—a look which is a toss-up between Hitler and a famous North Korean dictator, depending on how gung-ho the 'chief stylist' (that would be me) is with the scissors!

DB, who insists he only wants a little bit off the back, has taken a fair bit of persuasion to keep his appointment, but eventually, I tie him—sorry—sit him on a chair and try to ease his disquiet i.e. abject terror!

'Been anywhere recently on your holidays?' I say, employing one of my best hairdresser's chat lines.

'Fat chance,' grumbles DB.

'Doing anything nice at the weekend,' I continue as I brandish the kitchen scissors in readiness.

'Just be quiet and get on with it!' DB mutters, gripping the sides of the chair until his knuckles turn white.

'You'll soon look like a new man,' I say reassuringly.

'Yeh, but what new man?' DB says in a doom-laden voice. 'Bart Simpson? Elmer Fudd? Kevin the Minion?'

'I'm hoping for George Clooney,' I say dreamily, drifting into a brief fantasy of George and me on a Caribbean Island somewhere......

I reluctantly snap back to reality. 'Just put your head down and let me have a go,' I say, abandoning the hairdresser niceties. 'What can be so difficult about cutting in a straight line?'

'Exactly! I've seen you cut a loaf!' reasons DB. 'A dog's hind leg is straighter.'

I set to with the scissors, and for the first few snips, all goes to plan...

Then I get to a tricky bit, and a small chunk disappears in front of my eyes.

'Whoops!' I say before I can stop myself.

'What! What have you done? Why are you saying whoops!' DB turns his head away sharply, and the tip of the scissors digs into his neck.

'Aaargh!' he screams, 'That's my jugular! Is there blood? Am I bleeding? There's blood, isn't there?' he yells melodramatically.

'You're fine,' I say, 'I hardly touched you; now sit still, or there WILL be blood! Lots of it!'

I carry on and reach the bit that goes around his ear.

'You know this is what really happened to Van Gogh, don't you? One dodgy haircut by Mrs Van Gogh and snip! No ear!' I laugh loudly at my own joke.

'Yeh, not funny.' DB whimpers as the clip, clip of the blades, sounds loudly in his ear'oles.

At last, my creation is done.

'Would sir like to look in the mirror?' I ask, employing more of my hairdresser lingo.

Then I catch sight of the damage. The back of DB's head is, shall we say, less George Clooney and more pudding bowl. Perhaps a mirror isn't a good move.

'Actually, forget that; it looks lovely,' I say quickly, but DB isn't fooled. He snatches the mirror out of my hand and visibly blanches.

'What have you done!' he yells. 'I look like that idiot from 'Dumb and Dumber'.

There's a pause while I shape a suitable reply.

'Well, now you come to mention it....'

He decides it's time to scarper before I do any more damage.

'No chance of a tip then!' I shout after him.

SILLINESS IN SUFFOLK

As Covid restrictions have recently been downgraded, my Dearly Beloved and I are away for a few days in Aldeburgh, Suffolk. A trip to nearby Southwold is suggested by the hotel receptionist so I grab the car keys and make for the door.

'Hang on a minute,' says DB, 'I just want to check how far it is on Google Maps.'

'I'm afraid we don't have particularly good reception here, sir,' warns the receptionist, 'but it isn't far.'

DB is not one to take advice easily, so there follows a lot of very heated huffing and puffing and furious stabbing of the phone screen as he tries to get the map app to work. Just as I think I might have to force-feed him another of his blood pressure tablets, he exclaims in delight, 'Got it! And look, it's only just up the road; we can walk there!'

'Are you sure?' I question. 'I didn't think it was that near?'

'Well, look for yourself,' he says and triumphantly shows me the screen, which sure enough has a red position marker and then a blue dot almost next to it which says Southwold.

'We'll be there in no time,' he says breezily.

As Geography has never been my strong point, I capitulate, and off we set.

Now, I am wearing a brand-new pair of leather trainers along with a pair of clapped-out old socks which have had the stuffing knocked out of them by innumerable washes, so it's not long before the trainers have eaten the socks which now lie in a vicious lump under each heel. That means that the unyielding back of the new trainers is rubbing my heels raw, so it's not the pleasant coastal walk I had in mind.

DB is striding ahead so energetically, courtesy of the medical profession having fitted a pair of brand-new stents last month, that I hate to spoil his fun, but eventually, I can stand the agony no longer and, limping like Long John Silver with a bad attack of woodworm, I whimper, 'How much further is it?'

'Oh, can't be far now,' DB throws airily over his shoulder as I hobble on behind. Twenty minutes later, I'm emulating the grandchildren on a long car journey. 'Are we nearly there yet?' I whine.

'Not sure,' replies DB, who is now beginning to doubt even himself.

'Look at your phone again and check how far we've gone,' I beg, 'my heels are like two lumps of raw meat here.'

DB gets out his phone to check the map he used at the start of this mega marathon. I look over his shoulder and immediately spot the problem. In all his earlier frantic stabbing of the screen to find Southwold, he had dropped a pin not far from the town, which he had taken to be our position at the hotel.

I grab his phone and, eschewing the DB approach of—if I prod the screen hard enough and often enough, it will give me the answer I need—I check the distance. Calmly. Like a sane person would.

Southwold is, in fact, 16.3 miles away or 5 hours and 20 minutes walking time. A crow flying, even without new trainers and rogue socks, would think twice before setting off! 5 hours and 20 minutes! I turn on my (bleeding) heel and head back to the car.

***

So, we DRIVE to Southwold and have a walk (or a hobble, in my case) around the pretty town, but as expected, it's not long before DB is demanding an afternoon cup of tea and a scone.

'The Swan Hotel is meant to be nice,' I suggest. 'Let's go there.'

'As long as it's nearby,' replies DB, who is like a man possessed when he wants a scone.

It takes some time to find it, so DB is acting like he's in the final stages of malnutrition by the time we sit at a table. Unfortunately, as people are still reluctant to venture out, the place is like the Marie Celeste of tea rooms, with not even a glimpse of any serving staff. We wait so long that DB is in danger of fitting into his jeans before a waiter finally flits past the table.

'Excuse me!' DB calls. 'Can we order, please?'

'Certainly, sir,' he replies, 'because of Covid precautions, you just need to scan the QR code on the table,' and with that, he disappears back into the Bermuda Triangle for waiters.

'What the heck is a QR code?' DB rants. 'All I want is a scone!'

'It's that square scribble on the table,' I explain. 'You need to scan it with your phone. The order is automatically transferred to the kitchen, and then they'll bring it to us.'

DB tuts loudly and mutters something about 'stupid technology' and then takes his mobile and wafts it over the code as if he's scanning a packet of digestives. Not surprisingly, nothing happens. He adjusts the position of the phone slightly and tries again.

'You're waiting for a bleep, aren't you?'

He looks at me as if to say, 'What if I am?'

'You're not in flaming Waitrose,' I say in exasperation, 'you need to scan the code, like you're taking a photo!'

DB looks at me as if I'm mad. 'Why would I want a photo of a code? I want a scone and a cup of tea!'

'Let me do it,' I say, but DB is in full stubborn mode by now.

'No, I'll do it!' he says and scans the QR code. An order page appears on the screen.

'Right, this is more like it,' he says, salivating at the thought of a fruit scone coming his way. Sadly, it's not to be, as scones don't seem to feature on the menu.

'Ridiculous,' he rages, 'Call themselves a hotel! What hotel doesn't sell scones!'

'Well, clearly, this one,' I reply. 'Just order the tea.'

DB ticks the box next to 'breakfast tea', and the message, 'Your order has been taken,' appears on the screen.

'I'll have Earl Grey, please,' I say.

DB ticks the box next to Earl Grey tea and nothing happens.

He tries again, and still nothing happens.

Then his patience goes, which is a sure sign that the jabbing finger is about to be employed. He jabs, jabs, jabs at the screen. Still, no Earl Grey appears.

'Right, Earl Grey seems to be as mythical as the scones round here, so you'll have to have builder's tea like me,' he declares and jabs the appropriate box. Nothing.

'Give me strength!' DB yells, and the jabbing goes into overdrive. He's about to lob the phone across the room when

I wrestle it from his hand and try to make sense of what's going wrong.

Just at that moment, the phantom waiter reappears.

'Excuse me, sir,' he says apologetically, 'but you appear to have ordered 23 cups of tea. Are you sure you want that many?'

I burst into laughter but as DB's mouth is pursed like a cat's bottom, he's obviously not finding it as funny.

'No, just two cups, thank you,' I reassure him.

DB, with one last ditch attempt, adds, 'And a scone would be nice.'

The waiter looks at this techno-phobic old fossil and replies, 'Sorry sir, we don't do scones.'

***

For our last day, we decide to take a trip to Sutton Hoo— DB's choice—because clearly, if there's anything going to make a holiday go with a swing, it's a visit to an Anglo-Saxon burial ground.

'Come on, you'll enjoy it,' says DB, noticing that I'm not exactly jumping with joy at the prospect. 'It's only just down the road.'

'So is Sizewell nuclear reactor,' I reply, 'but I don't fancy a trip there either!' but it falls on conveniently deaf ears.

We arrive, park the car, and take our place in the never-ending entry queue. Covid precautions mean they are staggering the entry, so it's a long wait. We've only crept halfway along the queue when my Dearly Beloved decides that he needs to answer the call of nature.

'You should have gone before we left,' I say sternly, sounding like my mother. I send him off in search of a loo while I keep our place in the queue.

Time passes, and he's still not back. By this time, I'm at the top of the queue and in danger of missing our entry slot, so I ring him to ask what on earth he's doing.

'Waiting in a queue,' he says.

'No, I'm waiting in a queue.'

'Well, I'm waiting in a queue too. The queue for the loo.'

'All right, Wordsworth,' I say. 'You need to get back here, pronto; we're about to go in.'

'But I've not been yet.'

'Too bad,' I say unsympathetically.

A couple of minutes later I see DB hurrying back as fast as a full bladder allows.

We go through the gate and into the main complex.

'Right, I'm off to find another loo,' says DB and rushes off as fast as his crossed legs let him.

'Hurry up. I'll be ready for burial myself at this rate,' I call after him.

He's soon back again with the devastating news that the only other toilet is out of use because of social distancing problems. The only thing for it is a quick beetle around the burial site (result!) and then back through the exit to the original queue.

We follow the sign saying 'To the Burial Mounds', with DB now employing a kind of desperate knock-kneed shuffle. Soon, we're in a densely wooded area with a narrow path leading through it.

'It's no good, I can't go on,' says DB like some out-of-work Drama Queen. 'I'm going to have to nip behind this tree; keep a lookout.'

'Really?' I say, 'Near a sacred burial ground? Isn't that going to incur the wrath of Woden or whoever the Anglo-Saxon big cheese is? Could be dicing with death here, dear.'

But I'm talking to thin air as DB has disappeared behind a large tree.

Just at that moment I look behind me. A mobility scooter has appeared at the start of the path but it's a long way back, so I think nothing of it.

Big mistake.

This thing is like the formula one of granny-peds. Before I can blink, it's heading for us fast.

'Hurry up! There's a mobility scooter coming,' I warn.

'Not a lot I can do about that,' replies DB through a deep sigh of relief.

'Wee faster!'

'Pointless saying that to a man of my age!' exclaims DB.

'Well, try! This thing is turbocharged!'

'I've started, so I'll finish!' he says, as if on Mastermind.

Just as the mobility scooter draws level, DB re-emerges and says loudly, 'No, definitely no burial mounds there.' The Lewis Hamilton of mobility scooters throws him such a disapproving look that there's no chance he's been fooled for a minute.

We carry on to the burial ground, DB now with a skip in his step. This renowned archaeological site, Britain's answer to Tutankhamun, consists of a few lumps in the ground, and that's it, nothing more. I can't believe we've gone through all that stress for what resembles a badly laid lawn. Perhaps a trip to Sizewell would have been the better option after all.

STAND BACK!

Up until Covid captivity, my idea of gardening was to deadhead the occasional pansy while sipping a large G and T, but now I'm like a veritable Charlie Dimmock, well, apart from the bra size!

I'm surveying a really scruffy bit of lawn under a crab apple tree when inspiration strikes. What this needs is a little gravel bed to solve the problem!

I discuss it with DB, the under-gardener, who'd normally rather donate a kidney than have anything to do with a trowel, but surprisingly, his eyes light up as he sees the opportunity for a new 'project'. Now, my idea is to dig up the scruffy bit of grass and chuck some pea shingle on it, but no, Capability Brown has other ideas.

'So, here's what we need to do: dig down a couple of feet, pour some concrete footings, level the soil, sink the edging bricks, fill the....'

'Stop!' I yell. 'You'll be building a folly and installing a lake next; all we need is a bag of stones!' But no, DB is now in full Ground Force mode!

We drive to the newly opened garden centre for not just one, but SEVERAL bags of stones.

Here lies the problem. DB, with his dicky ticker, can't lift the bags onto the trolley; I, a puny weakling, can't either, so we have to find someone to help.

I eventually find an assistant who is stacking some huge wooden fence panels. He is lost in his own little world, meticulously sorting the panels into height order, so I say politely, 'Excuse me.' Nothing. I repeat it. Still no response. So, I muster my best stage voice, the product of three years of intensive training at a prestigious Drama College, 'EXCUSE ME!' The poor man jumps with fright, lets go of his carefully sorted stack of fencing panels, and we both watch in horror as, one by one, they clatter about his ears like a giant pack of cards. Lucky to escape serious injury, he abandons the scene of devastation at his feet and, dredging up the remnants of his customer service training, says through gritted teeth, 'How can I help you?'

Deciding it would be best not to mention his near-death experience, I explain that we need some help with the bags of stones.

Now, he's obviously read and digested the Coronavirus Health and Safety Manual because he urges me to keep my distance with an outstretched arm and a stern, 'STAND BACK, Madam!' as he hefts the bags onto one of those long-based trolleys for us.

The job done, I go to push the trolley when out shoots the extended arm again, with another barked order to, 'STAND BACK, Madam!' until he has safely distanced himself.

I can now take control of the trolley, but as it's laden with enough stones to build Heathrow's 4th runway and probably

243

its fifth and sixth, it's bloomin' heavy and reluctant to move. I give it one almighty push....and ram it into the back of his ankles.

Seeing him grimace painfully, I say, 'Oh, my goodness, I'm so sorry!' and instinctively walk towards him to see if he's alright.

'STAND BACK!' he yells with passion and employs the stiff arm again like a fully paid-up member of the Nazi party. I have a suspicion that this time, he's less concerned that I might be a Covid carrier than with the very real possibility that, somehow or other, this mad woman wants to do him in.

Fearing we're likely to mow down any customer between here and the exit, he insists, 'I'll take the trolley to the checkout for you,' and leaves DB and I traipsing behind him like two naughty children who've just been told off.

We arrive at the checkout, and the queue is almost twice around the shop.

It's a loooong wait, but at last, we pay for the stones, and I ask the till operator if there is someone who might help us get the stones into the car.

'Well, we're short-staffed, but I'll try for you,' she says and gets on the tannoy.

She has just said, 'Someone will be with you shortly,' when I see a familiar figure, limping from third-degree trolley injuries, approaching the till. It's our very own trainee-Hitler. He stops in his tracks when he sees us, incredulous that we're still here.

'Hi, it's us again!' I say cheerfully.

'So I see, Madam,' he replies, breaking out in a cold sweat.

He takes a deep breath, extends the arm, which must be suffering repetitive stress syndrome by now, and wearily issues the customary warning, 'STAND BACK' before trundling the trolley to our car.

Later that day, DB shouts from the garden, 'We're going to need another bag of stones.'

Think we'll find a different garden centre.

TELLY TALES

I suppose one of the dangers of lockdown is becoming 'square-eyed', as my mother used to say, if I watched too much telly. Well, our darling son isn't helping one bit! Thinking that the 'OLDS' might be incarcerated for months yet, he's been really thoughtful and bought us a very swish, bang-up-to-date television, which arrived on the doorstep as a fabulous surprise.

The one snag is that due to social distancing, John Lewis doesn't offer their usual set up service, so they ring the bell and then scarper before we can ask any questions. This leaves DB and I—winners of the 2020 Technophobe prize—with this enormous chunk of advanced technology to get up and running.

Not being technological 'whiz kids'—nor even 'whiz codgers'—we know this is going to be a challenge. We spend the first half hour just looking in stupefaction at the so called 'Easy Set Up' diagrams provided.

'Easy set up!' explodes DB as he turns the diagram upside down to see if that makes more sense. 'The essential words, "Only if you work for NASA," seem to be missing,' he adds grumpily.

He gets on all fours and squeezes his bulk between the heavy TV unit and the wall (no mean feat after 4 weeks of lockdown comfort eating) and starts plugging in leads willy-nilly.

'Try that,' he says.

I press the zapper.

Nothing.

Like a tetchy old school telephonist, he yanks out one set of cables and plugs in another.

'Try that.'

Nothing.

This goes on for some while.

'Press another button,' he complains, 'Press all of them! My knees are knackered, and I'm so squashed I can't breathe!'

He tries changing position but ends up in a worse position than before, lying on one hip with one leg bent, one outstretched, and the sharp corner of the TV unit sticking in the old gut bucket. A semi-impaled corpulent contortionist comes to mind. But I decide telling him that, probably wouldn't improve his mood any.

'I bet Victorian chimney boys weren't as cramped as I am right now!' he grumbles.

After a few more random efforts and a fair amount of abuse aimed at John Logie Baird, we eventually get a picture. Now all we have to do, is connect the sky box to the

TV, and we're good to go, but by this time, DB is ready to put a brick through it, brand new or not, so I suppose that's going to be my job. Tune in soon (see what I did there!) for the next thrilling episode of TV Tales!

TELLY TALES—PART 2

Welcome back to TV Tales. You'll remember that I was not so much volunteered as 'voluntold' to tune the TV to the sky box, as DB's nerves could take no more, so it's a simple choice: give it a go or face the prospect of Radio 4's 'Gardeners Question Time' for the foreseeable.

The Easy Start-Up guide, which, as we know, is anything but, gives no clue how you do this, so it's another head-scratcher.

I go to Professor Google and type in, 'Please help a numpty get the telly working,' and follow the instructions.

1. Go to settings - done

2. Go to network - done

3. Type in password - not done.

Password? What password? Password for what?

Go back to Google and type in 'Connect Sky to TV.'

Same advice.

Go back to Google and type in 'Connect router to TV.'

Same advice.

Go back to Google and type in 'Remedies for soaring blood pressure'.

Give up for health reasons.

Sit there glumly looking at brand new, swish telly, silently thumbing its nose at us.

Thankfully, number one son FaceTimes.

'How's the new TV?' he asks.

I 'fess up that there's a problem.

'Flip the screen and let me see it,' he suggests.

'Flip the TV screen? How do I do that?' I ask.

'Your phone screen, Mum! You're such a dinosaur!'

I do as I'm told (note the parent/ child role reversal).

'Right, this is what you do. Switch the router off at the wall, wait for 5 minutes, then reboot everything.' He says it V-E-R-Y S-L-O-W-L-Y as if talking to someone not quite right in the head. No comments.

Now, sadly for DB, the router switch is behind the hall table. Is this ringing a bell?

Guess who has to squeeze his girth behind yet another piece of heavy furniture?

My Dearly Beloved.

Guess who's not a happy camper?

Ditto.

But, hey presto, after a new set of contortions on DB's part, it works! The Sky box springs to life, and all is right with the world.

'You'll love the new TV,' number one son says excitedly, 'You can get Amazon Prime, Netflix, stream videos, use the apps, all sorts of things,' and then happily rings off, satisfied he's dragged the oldsters into the 21st century.

We go to the Home Screen, which displays a bewildering range of high-tech wizardry. There's a momentary pause, then we look at each other, shrug, and tune into 'Coronation Street'.

That sums it up, really!

THE FROZEN WASTES

It's Sod's law that the very time there's a food crisis, the freezer in the garage packs up. Of course, being in the garage, you don't know it's packed up until it's too late. I open the door and find a freezer full of fermented slush. DB, at the sight of his beloved ice cream stash melting into gloopy puddles, is bereft. He doesn't give two hoots about the frozen meat, fish and veg that have also given up the ghost. NOTHING messes with his daily ice cream intake!

'Quick!' he yells. 'Get online to Curry's and order a new freezer; my mint choc chip is mush!'

Knowing he's in danger of turning feral, I do as I'm told.

'Good news!' I say, 'They can deliver one on Friday.'

'Friday? FRIDAY?' splutters DB, hyperventilating. 'That's no good. Try Amazon; they do next-day delivery.'

'Yeah, not for freezers, love,' I reason. 'You're not going to get one of those in a padded envelope and push it through the letterbox!

'Don't see why not,' mutters DB, as he cradles the ice cream box lovingly with a tear in his eye.

'Well, how about a yoghurt instead?' I suggest.

'No thanks!'

'Some rice pudding?'

'Definitely not!'

'Well, a nice bowl of custard? Custard's nice.'

I can see that he's close to meltdown - pardon the pun - so I shut up and get on with disposing of the defrosted food. I'm just about to chuck a semi-frozen loaf of bread in the bin when DB stops me.

'Don't throw that away,' he says, 'That'll do the birds. I'll throw it on the lawn for them.'

'Good idea,' I say and carry on clearing up the mess that's left. A few minutes later, I look out of the window and see two valiant pigeons in serious danger of dislocating their necks as they struggle to pick up an entire slice of frozen bread! Never one to waste energy, DB hadn't broken the bread up into small pieces but just lobbed the whole loaf onto the grass!

One of the pigeons stops struggling with the enormous slice in his beak and looks at his pal as if to say, 'Give us a hand here, mate; this thing weighs a ton!'

The other pigeon gives it a go. 'Are these people nuts? I've knackered my neck lifting this! As the pigeon flies, how far is the nearest hospital?'

I go and find DB. 'Why didn't you break up the bread for the birds,' I ask. 'They're struggling with a massive slice of frozen bread out there, poor things.'

'Thought they'd appreciate a square meal,' chuckles DB. 'You know, slice of bread, square, square meal....'

I look at him pityingly. Self-isolation has addled his brain.

YOU CANNOT BE
SERIOUS

A FISHY BUSINESS

The grandchildren are coming for a sleepover and as always, we try to find some fun activities to do.

'Let's go magnet fishing,' DB suggests.

'Magnet fishing?' I ask in confusion. 'Never heard of a magnet fish! Does that come with microchips?'

'Idiot,' DB scoffs at my ignorance. 'You throw these really big magnets into the water and see what you catch.'

'Very little, I would think. Probably knock out any possible fish, throwing ruddy great magnets at them,' I say, still in blissful ignorance.

'No, you don't understand, numpty!' DB scoffs again. 'You're not catching fish; you're catching bits of metal!'

'Random bits of old metal?'

'Well, yes,' DB says awkwardly, as even to him, it is beginning to sound like a crackpot idea.

'Thrilling,' I continue sarcastically. 'And what happens if you "catch" a shopping trolley or a rusty bike?'

'Well, you have to keep it. You're not allowed to throw it back,' DB answers, shuffling shiftily.

'Or an old boiler?' I continue, warming to my theme.

'The only old boiler we'll end up with is you, dear,' he quips.

I don't find that terrifically amusing, and neither am I thrilled by the prospect of becoming the local 'Steptoe and Son,' but DB is completely up for it, so...

The day dawns. The grandkids are here. We've borrowed three enormously heavy magnets attached to meters and meters of rope, and off we set for the river.

Being novices at the sport, there are some teething problems.

The first bright idea is to pile all the magnets into one bag, which means they are now glued together so strongly that even Arnie Schwarzenegger would risk a hernia prising them apart. We all have a go, but they are not budging. In desperation, we form two lines and, with a kind of tug o' war set up, try hauling them apart with sheer brute force, much to the amusement of passers-by. But the fun doesn't end there!

The ropes attached to the magnet are now in an enormous tight knot. We manage to free one of the magnets while Grandpa sets to untangling the others. Twenty minutes later, the kids are fed up waiting, and Grandpa, wishing he'd kept his copy of 'Knots for Boy Scouts,' is still untangling the rope.

As one magnet is free to use, I suggest the kids take turns to chuck it in the river and see what they can find. Isla has the first go but forgets to let go of the rope and is in danger of being dragged into the water along with the magnet! Toby is next but doesn't realise he is standing on the rope, so the magnet rebounds off a wooden barrier, nearly taking out both kneecaps. Zach, having witnessed his siblings' pathetic attempts, decides that swinging the magnet around his head like a frenzied hammer thrower should do the trick and nearly decapitates his sister. It is a flaming health and safety nightmare!

Meanwhile, Grandpa is still untangling the knot.

Zach has another go, this time with his sister out of harm's way, and launches the magnet deep into the water. Success! 'It must be something really big, grandma; I can't pull it out!' Zach yells excitedly. Zach and I pull the rope. Nothing. Zach, Toby, and I pull the rope. Nothing. Zach, Toby, Isla, and I all pull the ruddy rope. Nothing.

I expect at least a double-decker bus to rise majestically from the deep at any minute, but then I realise the heavy magnet has obviously wedged itself firmly in some underwater roots. Despite more frantic hauling on the rope, it doesn't budge.

Grandpa is still untangling the knot.

At last, after pulling like maniacs, the magnet suddenly releases itself, and the kids and I end up in an undignified pile on the riverbank like a bunch of second-rate Keystone Cops. There is a smattering of applause from some gathered bystanders who had no idea when they set off how entertaining a quiet walk by the river could be. I look up at the sky. Dark clouds have gathered, and it is beginning to rain. 'Shall we give this up, children?' I ask, looking at their forlorn faces. 'YES!' they all chorus in relief.

'At last!' yells Grandpa in triumph, holding up the untangled magnet, 'I've unravelled the knot!' But he is talking to thin air—the kids and I have made a beeline for the car.

Grandpa tosses up whether he should throw the magnet or himself into the river.

A HORROR STORY

We're both suffering a touch of PTSD, having just spent two nights in a B&B that rivals Bates Motel. The plan was to meet up with family for the weekend, go to the Ashbourne Show, which is the highlight of the Derbyshire agricultural scene, and have a jolly good time. Of course, most of the Midlands thought the same, so getting accommodation was a nightmare—in more ways than one, as it turns out!

We arrive at a tall, narrow terrace house and ring the bell. The door slowly creaks open, and we're greeted by a severe-looking landlady who has obviously graduated from the Mrs Danvers School of Housekeepers: civil on the outside but plotting dastardly deeds on the inside.

'I'll show you to your room,' she says with an evil smile, 'I've put you in the attic.' We wait for a crazy 'mwah-ha-ha' to follow, but she's obviously lulling us into a false sense of security.

Now, it's the kind of terrace house where you reach the stairs by going through the dining room, so I can't help noticing that the table is set for two, yet we've seen neither sight nor sound of any other human.

She leads us to the landing, which has two doors, and opens one, which has a flight of precipitous stairs leading upwards.

'Your room is up there,' she says, again just stopping short of a maniacal cackle, and shuts the door firmly behind us.

For a moment, I wonder if that means we're now incarcerated for all time in the attic room, never to see daylight again.

'If there's a rocking chair up there, DON'T SIT IN IT!' I warn DB, who's in front of me.

We climb the stairs to find a narrow room with sloping ceilings just ripe for giving you a concussion.

'I bet that's her cunning plan,' I say as my head slams into the ceiling for the second time. 'She renders us unconscious then chops us up a-la-Sweeney Todd to feed to the phantom dinner companion.'

DB swallows nervously.

Later, we venture out to meet up with the others. As we walk through the dining room again, the two place settings have been cleared, yet there is still no sign of another person.

Cue spooky music—Dun, Dun, Duuuuun!

'Right, that does it,' I say to DB, 'We've got to get back well before the witching hour. Heaven knows what happens to Norma Bates at midnight, but I want to be in our room with the door firmly locked!'

We return home at around 11.00. Thankfully, all is quiet. There is no sign of Norma, so we tiptoe up the stairs to the landing. Then…a near disaster.

DB leads the way and, in the gloom, is about to yank open the door to the attic when I notice that it isn't the door to the attic.

'No, stop!' I whisper in panic.

'What?' he whispers back.

'That's the wrong door!'

'No, it isn't!'

'Yes, it is! That's the landlady's room!'

'Rubbish,' hisses DB.

'I'm telling you. She's the sort who sleeps in a coffin with an oversized bread knife under her pillow!' I continue. 'So, unless you've got a wooden stake and a Tesco's pack of garlic handy, I'd take my word for it.'

DB gulps and quickly lets go of the handle.

We barely sleep a wink all night, waiting for Ashbourne's Rose West to appear any minute wielding the aforementioned bread knife, so we're relieved when morning dawns and we can set off for the Ashbourne show.

On our return in the evening, we open the front door for our noses to be assailed by the acrid smell of 'something' cooking. I use the term 'something' because it defies description. Imagine the aroma of something that has died, festered in a swamp for a few months, and is now simmering in its own juice. Like that.

I look towards the table, and yet again, there are two places set, but no hint of anyone else here, only the rhythmic sound of chopping! Was it the remains of the last unfortunate tenants? Are we next on the chopping block?

We scurry off upstairs, lock the door, and decide to leave at the crack of dawn before we become the next day's plat du jour.

A TIGHT SQUEEZE!

We've been pretending we're oligarchs all weekend—staying on the Seaborn Yacht in London Docklands to celebrate our cousin Sue's birthday.

DB has dusted off his best dicky bow, and I've dug out the family pearls (fake) in the vain hope we might fit in with the superyacht clientele. DB even goes the whole hog with matching cummerbund.

'Not sure that's going to fit,' I say as I see him struggle to fasten it around his ample girth. But nothing daunted, DB takes a deeper breath and continues the fight.

'Give it up, love,' I continue, looking at his flushed face which now has a hint of overripe aubergine.

But I see that stubborn glint in his eye that says, 'Never!' So, he struggles on, getting more and more frustrated by the impossible task.

A couple of minutes later, there is a shout of triumph.

'Done it!'

But pride comes before a fall, and just as DB turns round to view in the mirror the spoils of his personal war, there's a loud twang, and the wayward cummerbund shoots across the room—or should that be cabin?

'That nearly had my eye out then!' I say, ducking to avoid the sartorial Exocet.

264

'Well, see if you can do any better!' DB replies peevishly.

I retrieve the cummerbund, position myself behind him, and try to wrap it around his waist. But the winter months of comfort eating have taken their toll, so, short of placing my foot on the small of his back and yanking with all my might like a Victorian maid tying the laces of her Ladyship's corset, it ain't happening.

'This is ridiculous!' I say. 'You'll have to go without.'

'All right,' he says reluctantly, 'Help me with my bow tie then.'

But the bow tie, apparently having seen the trauma his mate, the cummerbund, has just been put through, comes out in solidarity and also refuses to fasten.

Thankfully, there's an adjustment at the back, but when this is employed, the tie is too loose. So, DB has a choice: strangulation or brewer's droop.

Safe to say neither look is going to cut the mustard with the yachting elite. Oh well, back to jeans and a jumper tomorrow!

A WAVE OF EMBARRASSMENT

The day starts by trying to find my Dearly Beloved's National Trust card, which is missing from his wallet. Actually, it isn't missing, it's in his wallet all along—just in a different part of his wallet. Of course, we don't discover this until every drawer and cupboard in the house has been ransacked. Twice.

'You said you'd looked in your wallet,' I say, taking several deep breaths.

'I did,' DB replies, 'just not in that part of my wallet.'

I count to ten.

We arrive at Scotney Castle. The hunt for the great missing NT card, which wasn't really missing, means that by now, the car park is chokka, so we're directed to the overflow car park. As DB parks the car, I walk towards the castle and spot a very friendly car park attendant waving at the bottom of the car park.

I wave back and carry on walking.

He waves again.

I wave back.

He sidesteps and waves again, this time more frantically.

I wave back.

'For the love of Mike, what are you doing?' rebukes DB, who has now caught me up. 'Stop waving!'

'Why,' I say. 'He's being friendly. The least I can do is wave back.'

'He's waving at the car that's behind you, you doughnut. It can't get past because you're walking in the middle of the road!'

'Oh, well, he should have said, instead of waving like a lunatic!' I say.

I try to regain a modicum of dignity as DB yanks me roughly to the side to let the car pass, but the sight of two teenage faces through the back window creased up with laughter at the crackpot-waving woman tells me it is futile.

'Blimey, you're embarrassing sometimes,' DB says.

Later, we stop for an ice cream. I'm not a huge fan of ice cream, but the shop here sells lemon sorbet, which I love.

DB is just about to take a lick when I say, 'Wait! I never have an ice cream; let me take a picture to record this moment for posterity.'

'Really?' DB sighs, desperate to get his choppers around his mint choc chip. Just as I click the picture, DB can wait no longer and dives into his cone, nudging my arm as he does so. There is a moment of frantic juggling between phone and ice cream, but my lemon sorbet loses out, and before you can say, 'Just One Cornetto,' it hits the deck.

'Bad luck, old girl,' DB says unsympathetically through a mouthful of ice cream.

Not certain that I can stand any more mishaps, I persuade him that we should head back to the car park.

'Ok,' he says, 'But remember.'

'What?'

'No waving!'

BRING ME SOME FIGGY PUDDING!

We had a lovely Christmas with the family coming to us for Christmas dinner. They brought some goodies over, including a Christmas pud.

Now, I know this is controversial, but to me, Christmas pudding is a culinary catastrophe. I don't care if Mary Berry, Marcus Waring, and even Heston Bloomin' Heck got together and made one. I wouldn't touch it with a ten-foot barge pole!

DB on the other hand, loves, nay adores, the stuff. At the mere mention of the word, he's salivating like a Pavlovian dog.

Anyway, it bothers me not a jot when Craig, our son, declares, after scoffing a surfeit of turkey and trimmings, that he's too full to eat any pudding.

DB says nothing, but his face is a picture. No, actually, make that a masterpiece. Imagine Edvard Munch's 'The Scream', and you've got a good approximation of it. There is no sound, just a face slowly morphing in horror at the thought of no Christmas pudding.

To be honest, he's a bit 'Bah Humbug' about most things Christmas, but when Christmas pudding is mentioned, he can out-hark any Herald Angel, Jingle every Bell going, and Ding Dong Merrily with the best of them.

The problem is, as we hadn't actually bought the pudding, he's too polite to say: 'Stuff it, you might be too full, but my pudding stomach is ready and waiting—so bring on the plum duff!'

'We'll have it tomorrow, Dad, when you come to ours,' says the son and heir. Everyone else gives a huge sigh of relief, but DB manages only a begrudging grunt as he begins counting down the hours to Boxing Day.

The next day dawns, and DB is already salivating at the thought of finally sinking his gnashers into some rich, fruity pudding. We've just got into the car when my mobile rings. It's Craig.

'Sorry to tell you, but I've just tested positive for Covid, so it's best you stay at home.'

DB can't believe it. His chance of a bowlful of Christmas pud has once more disappeared into thin air.

'What's a dose of Covid when there's Christmas pudding at stake!' he says, staying put. 'It's not as if it's Typhoid, or Black Death, or Beri Beri.'

'Don't be ridiculous! Get out of the car!' I scold.

'But my Christmas pudding...' he mutters, as disappointed as a kid who's just found out there's no Santa.

'You can have some next year,' I say, but it's no consolation. DB's Christmas is ruined...

Today we go shopping in Tesco. DB is ahead of me when he suddenly stops in his tracks. I just manage to avoid running the shopping trolley into the back of his legs, only to realise he is transfixed. His face is beaming with joy, and his eyes are alight with excitement. Right in front of us is a shelf filled with cut-price Christmas Puddings. The fact they are LARGE Christmas Puddings for EIGHT people, and I don't touch the stuff, doesn't deter DB one bit.

He bounds forward, elbows akimbo in case anyone dares to impede his way and grabs one from the shelf like a crazed contestant on Supermarket Sweep.

Later, he is not just in seventh heaven but eighth, ninth, and tenth heaven as he tucks into his Christmas Pudding. The one that feeds eight, I repeat, EIGHT people. Was he daunted? Not a bit of it! At last, he's full of good cheer. Not to mention Christmas Pudding!

CHARITY BEGINS AT HOME

I have been on a quest. Was it difficult? Let's just say that searching for the Holy Grail was a cinch in comparison. The quest? Finding a new pair of shoes for a wedding. I've looked high and low, but like the ugly sisters, my plates of meat just won't fit in anything.

Eventually, I crack it—a vibrant coral colour, a comfy fit. Sorted.

I get home, footsore and weary, and drop the shoes in their bag by the door while I make a much-needed cuppa.

My Dearly Beloved shouts, 'Just going for a haircut, back soon.'

He's back in an hour, and I decide to show him my new shoes, but they're not where I left them. *Funny,* I think; *I'm sure I left them by the door.*

'Have you seen my new shoes?' I ask DB.

'No,' he says.

'The ones in the bag by the door.'

'Nope. Not seen th...' DB suddenly stops in his tracks. His face pales, and he stutters, 'W-were they near that bag of old clothes?'

'Yes,' I reply.

'The clothes for the charity shop.'

'Yes,' I reply again.

He gulps audibly.

'You didn't!'

Silence

'YOU HAVEN'T!!!'

Silence

'I have.'

I'm speechless. Well, almost.

'You complete dipstick! You've taken my brand-new shoes to the charity shop!'

'Well, I thought I'd save you a trip,' he says lamely.

I'm fuming.

'Get in the car.' I say through gritted teeth.

'But....' he continues, trying to dredge up another excuse.

'Stop! No more words,' I say, marching him up the garden path.

'If we don't get to that shop before those shoes are sold....' I threaten, but I need to say no more. We hit warp speed as DB imagines, in grisly detail, the fate that awaits him.

We screech to a halt outside the charity shop like the local Cagney and Lacey and I dive through the door.

There, on a shelf, shining like a bright orange beacon amongst a sea of dingy, scuffed leather, are my beautiful shoes.

I grab them quickly and take them over to the counter.

'Ooh, aren't they lovely!' says the shop lady. 'And they're in such good condition—they're almost brand new!'

Almost? Bloomin' nerve! They ARE brand new! I think, outraged. Then, to add insult to injury, she says, 'That'll be £10.00, please!'

Brilliant, I think, they cost a fortune to start with, and now I've got to pay another tenner to get them back!

I explain what my nincompoop husband has done, and, realising I'm obviously lumbered with a dimwit, she takes pity on me and refuses the payment.

I give her a donation anyway and then spend the journey home wondering if the charity shop would like a nice new suit, DB size!

CHOO, CHOO!

'So, how about a trip on the Spa Valley steam train?' I say to my Dearly Beloved.

His eyes light up as sixty-odd years vanish in an instant, and he's a little boy again, playing with his Hornby train set.

'Ooh, yes, great idea,' he says with relish. 'I love steam trains! I always wanted to be a station master when I was a lad.'

A couple of minutes later, he's scrabbling through the contents of the kitchen drawer.

'What are you looking for?' I ask.

'Just the car keys,' he replies casually, but I'm suspicious. He's keenly eyeing up an old ARP whistle we keep in there. In the hands of a frustrated station master, that could cause chaos, I realise.

I slam the drawer shut quickly, spoiling his fun.

'Come on, we'll be late,'

DB grabs his hat. Of course, what he really wants is a station master's cap with lots of gold braid, but a rather battered Panama will have to do.

We arrive at the station and board the train. DB, in his element, walks up and down the corridor like Isambard Kingdom Brunel himself, inspecting the various carriages.

We're soon at the terminus, where the train stops for a few minutes.

After a visit to the Ladies, there's no sign of DB. I look up and down the platform. No DB. I look in the carriage where we were sitting. No DB. I even hover around the door to the gents like an out-of-work perv. No DB. Time is marching on, and the train will leave any minute.

The train whistle blows, and now I'm in a mad panic. What do I do now? Pull the emergency chain? Garrotte the driver? Tie myself to the tracks like a reject from a silent movie? I'm just about to throw myself on the mercy of the guard when the brim of a Panama hat emerges from the driver's cabin.

DB has somehow wangled his way into the train driver's good books and is being given a conducted tour!

'Was that you?' I say.

'What?' he replies innocently.

'Blowing the train whistle?'

'Might have been,' he says.

I drag him back to our carriage, and, exhausted by his adventure, he's soon asleep. I try engaging him in conversation to no avail. Only the words 'tea and cake' miraculously revive him, and when we arrive back at Tunbridge Wells, his feet hardly touch the ground as he strides off to find a tea shop.

Fine by me—I need to let off steam!

CINDERELLA AND THE NEW TRAINERS

Now, I don't know what your New Year's resolution is, but mine is to go power walking. Actually, this was last year's resolution, too, and surprisingly, it's one of the few resolutions I've ever kept. Unless, of course, you count, 'Never take out a gym membership' or 'Stop eating Brussels sprouts.' Anyway, if I'm going to keep it up, a new pair of trainers is a must.

We sally forth to the hell hole that is JD Sports–a shop that should carry a mental health warning. We're immediately confronted by a thronging mass of thuggish teenagers who apparently regard a trip to JD Sports as the pinnacle of their social life. They stand around in noisy, impenetrable groups, glued to their phones, occasionally glancing at some sports gear while obsessively texting their mate who is standing right next to them.

This circus is punctuated by the girls' screams of manic laughter as one of their male counterparts swaggers up and down the shop, doing something unsavoury with a pair of budgie smugglers.

I wonder briefly why the shop assistant isn't policing this behaviour, but one look at him and I realise he's of the same ilk.

'I'd like to try on these trainers, please, in size 6,' I say, handing him the one I've taken off the display stand.

He looks at me in disbelief, as if someone as decrepit as me has no business stepping foot in a sports shop, let alone buying something.

'Yeah. Not sure if we've got your size. Do you want to try that one on?' he says, pointing to the one I've got in my hand. I look at him incredulously.

'But these are a size 4,' I say.

'Yeah, like I say, not sure we've got a 6.'

DB and I exchange glances—obviously, we've got one of the elite JD sales teams here.

'Ok. How about this one?' I say, choosing another style.

'Do you want me to check if we've got a 6?' he says with about as much enthusiasm as if I'd asked him to undergo root canal treatment.

'Obvs,' I reply, wondering if a bit of 'yoof' vernacular might spur him into action.

He mutters something into his headset, inaudible to me, but probably along the lines of, 'There's an old coffin dodger here who wants to try on these trainers. Gawd knows why— she could croak any minute.'

The size 6's duly appear, and Happy Larry takes them out of the box. Then, I notice a slight snag.

'Er, you've given me two left feet,' I point out.

'Oh yeah,' he says, completely uninterested. 'Don't know what's happened there,' he says.

'Well, you've obviously had a customer with two right feet,' I quip.

He looks at me in confusion.

'Well, do you wanna try them on?' he says sulkily.

DB and I look at each other both thinking the same thing. Cheery Chops isn't a candidate for Mastermind.

'Not much point, is there really,' I point out, 'what with them both being for the same feet!'

'Suppose not,' he mumbles, clearly put out at my lack of cooperation. Then his face suddenly brightens.

'If you want them, you can have 50% off,' he declares cheerfully.

We burst into laughter, thinking he's finally found a sense of humour, but no—he's deadly serious!

'Not much of a bargain, though, is it, only being able to wear one, plus having to hop everywhere!' I say pointedly.

'Suit yourself,' he grumbles, tossing them back in the box, stroppy that I'd turned down his deal of the century.

In the hope of introducing some much-needed levity into the situation, I jest, 'Not even Cinderella had this much hassle!' but his moroseness is impenetrable.

I grab one last option from the display shelf. Miraculously, they have my size, as well as the added luxury of having a right AND left foot. I try them on, and they fit perfectly. I have one last stab at humour.

'Yay, they fit! I CAN go to the ball!' I say, but his face remains blank, as imaginary tumbleweed blows across the shop floor.

We pay for the trainers and are just about to leave the shop when I see some sports socks on a nearby stand.

'Oh, look!' I say to DB, who, as you can imagine, is thoroughly cheesed off with the whole shopping trip. 'I might get a pair of those.'

'Not unless you want to wear them in a Divorce Court,' he replies.

SOMETHING TO DIGEST!

My birthday treat is to see a show in London. I've also persuaded my Dearly Beloved to book a dinner reservation in the Brasserie opposite the theatre, thinking: a leisurely glass of prosecco, romantic candle-lit dinner, and stroll to the theatre. But no.

As we leave the house, DB, who's always chirpy at the prospect of food, asks, 'What time's our table booked for?'

'6.45,' I reply.

'You sure that's going to give us enough time?'

'Plenty', I reassure him. 'The show doesn't start 'til eight.'

Off we set for the restaurant, but we're not two miles down the road when sat nav disaster strikes again!

Faceless sat nav lady drones, 'Satellite connection lost,' then repeats, 'Satellite connection lost,' and so she continues until she's blue in the face–if she had a face. And if she did have a face, DB was itching to rearrange it.

We ditch technology and resort to a good old-fashioned map book. Alas, after a few map-reading glitches by yours truly (which do nothing to improve DB's mood), we don't arrive at the restaurant until seven o'clock.

As I check that the tickets are in my bag, I discover that I've mistaken the time; the show starts at 7.30 not 8.00. Now,

DB is already a touch ratty, but when I explain that he has even less time to devour his dinner than he thought, he becomes veritably thunderous.

The waiter arrives, and we order, explaining that we are due at the theatre in half an hour.

'There's nothing better than being able to savour a meal,' DB says sarcastically, fuming at the prospect of having to throw his pork belly down his throat without tasting it.

The first course arrives, and we hoover it up as fast as our ageing digestive systems can manage.

As the waiter clears our plates, and not realising that he is dicing with death, he utters the words that spell doom to DB's ears.

'I'm afraid you won't have time for a dessert, sir.'

DB is aghast at the sound of those words, but nothing, NOTHING, can separate my darling husband from his beloved puddings, so with a firm set of his shoulders, he says, 'Bring me your best chocolate nut sundae!'

'Is that wise?' I ask, looking at the clock.

Undaunted, DB polishes off his pud at breakneck speed, and with only minutes to spare, we get to our seats.

For the rest of the evening, the show is punctuated for me and most of the rest of the audience by strange rumblings and gurglings coming from the vicinity of DB.

'Why did you let me eat that pudding,' DB belches as we drive home. 'The sooner we get home, the better. I need some Alka-Seltzer, pronto!'

'Satellite connection lost,' sniggers faceless sat nav lady.

It's going to be a long night.

HAPPY NEW YEAR!

It's the first month of a new year, and I'm sure we're all hoping for a better and brighter 2021. Of course, it comes as no surprise that the Bundells end the last day of the ghastly year that was 2020 with a typical disastrous 'adventure'.

Now, we Scots love a good knees-up on New Year's Eve, or Hogmanay, as we call it. Sadly, my idea of a raucous Hogmanay these days goes something like this:

Get into PJs at the earliest opportunity.

12.00—quaff some Prosecco that I don't really want.

12.10—quaff some Gaviscon that I DO really want (having drunk the Prosecco.)

12.15—be tucked up in bed.

I remember the giddy days of my youth in Scotland when first footing didn't even start until after the chimes of midnight and, in comparison, glumly contemplate the dull prospect of the evening ahead.

'New Year's Eve is really boring when you're old,' I bemoan to my Dearly Beloved. 'I wish we could do something exciting.'

He thinks about this for a while and then comes up with the most ridiculous suggestion of the century, let alone 2020.

'Let's go for a picnic!' he says.

Yes, you read that right—a ruddy picnic. In December. When it's cold enough for even penguins to be poking their beaks outside and thinking, 'Nah, stuff it.'

'A picnic?' I splutter. 'In this weather?'

'Yes, come on, we'll wrap up warm, take a sandwich and some hot soup in a flask for lunch, and have a nice walk by the river.'

'That is just ten types of wrong,' I say but foolishly agree, so we set off muffled up like two out-of-work Himalayan Sherpas.

It begins well. The grass is crisp with frost, and bare branches stand starkly silhouetted against a winter sky. But this is the Bundells. You know it's not going to last.

The crisp ground soon becomes a swamp, and DB and I begin slip-sliding over the mud like a poor man's Torvill and Dean.

'Hold onto me!' I shout, but DB goes selectively deaf as he faces his own struggle to stay upright. He ploughs on, lurching like a Saturday night drunk, grabbing any spare piece of shrubbery as a handhold.

I'm now doing my pensioned-off Bambi-on-ice act with some ungainly skidding and lunging while facing, for the first time in over sixty years, the unappetising prospect of doing the splits.

DB, facing his own hazards, comes to a slight incline and decides to take a run at it but doesn't quite reach the summit before sliding back down. Trying to avoid the inevitable face plant in the mud, he employs some desperate windmilling of his arms, then glides seamlessly into a spin that Christopher Dean would be proud of and ends up facing the direction he just came from.

'Whose stupid idea was this,' I say through gritted teeth as I try to dodge his flailing arms and only just avoid a triple axel of my own.

'Stop whinging,' DB replies. 'You wanted to do something exciting. This is it.'

I spot a fallen log in the distance and lay down an ultimatum.

'Right, that log is as far as I'm going.'

We reach the log and, thankful that the gymnastics of the last half hour had come to an end, we eat lunch.

'Thank goodness for a rest,' I say gratefully, sipping some hot soup. And then the realisation strikes: we've got the joys of navigating the same mudslide on the return journey.

I'M A LUMBERJACK, AND I'M OK

It's a little-known fact that my Dearly Beloved once dreamed of emigrating to Canada to be a lumberjack. Well, dreams can come true—sort of.

The weather has been a mite chilly, to say the least, and with energy bills snapping at the heels of the bank balance like wild animals, DB has programmed the central heating not to come on until teatime which makes an afternoon cuppa and a browse of the newspaper seem like an Arctic sport. All that's missing is a sled and a team of huskies.

I'm sitting in the lounge watching frostbite developing in my extremities when DB breezes in.

'Brrrr! It's a bit parky in here,' he understates.

'Parky!' I exclaim. 'Parky? It's moved on from parky, past glacial to practically polar vortex!' I shiver. 'Even my thermals have given up the struggle and retired to Florida!'

'Well, no point in putting on the central heating when we've got a log burner,' says DB.

'Yeh, the slight snag with that, Ebenezer,' I point out. 'Log burners need logs, and we ran out a couple of days ago.'

'Well, why didn't you say?' he queries, possibly adding 'dimwit' under his breath.

DB goes online to order some logs. Now the observant amongst you will have noticed some words in that sentence which do not bode well—'DB' and 'goes online'. I have written oft of the horror stories that ensue when DB touches technology. Today is not much different. It doesn't take long before the exasperated tuts begin, then the frenzied jabbing at the touchscreen, followed by exasperated mutterings of 'this stupid iPad isn't working again.'

'By the way, make sure you order the right size of logs,' I remind him. 'They have to be small enough for a log burner.'

'Yeh, yeh,' he mutters while he continues to stab at the screen like a maniac.

'Success!' he eventually shouts, beaming as if he'd just discovered his very own Higgs boson. 'They're coming in the morning, so we'll soon be well stocked.'

The following day, as I'm donning multiple layers of clothing, I hear the distinctive rumble of the log truck. Throwing off the fleece-lined undies with gay abandon (can you say that these days?), I race downstairs to find DB in the driveway, looking somewhat irritated. In fact, I haven't seen him frown so much since he wondered if he'd left the chip pan on.

'What's the problem?' I ask, but it soon becomes apparent as I look past my Dearly Beloved to the mountain of logs that has just been dumped on the drive. Well, I say logs. These are semi-tree trunks. If one of the Three Little Pigs had built his house with these, the Big Bad Wolf would have given himself a double hernia blowing THAT lot down!

DB's fickle finger had sabotaged him again as he'd obviously missed the 'suitable for log burners' option and hit 'might fit a blast furnace if trimmed a bit' instead.

'Never mind, dearest,' I say chirpily, 'You can live out your boyhood dream after all. Get chopping!'

An hour later, DB has revisited his boyhood dream of being a Lumberjack and changed it to Chiropractor in the hope he may be able to find a cure for his bad back, his bad shoulder, his bad arm…

KITCHEN CHAOS

We're all familiar with Einstein's famous equation,

$$E = MC^2$$

Well, anyone who has had their kitchen renovated will also be familiar with this one:

Kitchen Refurb + Demolition=Temporary Insanity

The last time we decided to remodel the kitchen was at least twelve years ago, when both of our memories were a lot sharper; a time when we could remember where we had put things. However, on this occasion, it's a whole new ball game. So, a typical breakfast goes something like this:

Go into the bomb site, otherwise known as the kitchen, and put the kettle on.

Realise there are no tea bags.

Go to the living room, where, after meticulous planning on my part, everything that used to be in the kitchen cupboards now lives in a series of boxes behind the sofa.

Look into the box that should contain the tea bags.

Nothing.

Shout at Dearly Beloved— 'Where are the tea bags?'

'What teabags?' he shouts back.

'Any tea bags! THE tea bags!'

'In the study,' he shouts back as if I'd just asked the bleedin' obvious.

'Why the study?'

'Cos, that's where I put them.'

Take a deep breath.

'They're supposed to be in the yellow box behind the sofa.'

'Thought they were supposed to be in the blue box in the study.'

Take a deeper breath.

Find tea bags.

Make tea.

'Where's the bread?' I ask.

'In the bread bin.'

'Where's the bread bin?'

'Dunno. Wherever the bread is.'

Begin to steam.

'And the marmalade?'

'Dunno. Where did you put it?'

I know where I'd like to put it! I think.

Eventually, breakfast is made.

Look at the clock—lunchtime is now rapidly approaching.

'Where's the cheese?'.......

***

I've ordered a number of new kitchen appliances, all from different stores, so it can get confusing.

Two men arrive with a new machine. They take one look at the kitchen, which now resembles a scene from the Blitzkrieg, and say they'll leave it in the hallway. They begin to dash back to their van to escape the choking brick dust, when I realise something is amiss.

'You were supposed to collect the old machine,' I call after them.

'Don't think so, love.' They continue down the path.

'No, really, I organised pick up as well,' I insist.

He looks at a grubby bit of paper in his hand.

'Sorry love, it's got to be on the docket,' he waves his bit of paper.

'Well, check it again, please,' I say in an irritated voice.

'Nope, it's not here.'

'Are you sure?' I persist.

He walks back up the path and shoves 'the docket' under my nose. 'Now, this is the docket. See? Can you see it on the docket? No! Because-it's-not-on-the-docket,' he says slowly, as if explaining the theory of relativity to a backward two-year-old.

Tempted to take his docket and shove it somewhere very uncomfortable, I reply in my best school ma'am's voice, 'Well, I think you'll find your docket's wrong. I paid extra for delivery AND pickup, and if you look at MY docket, you'll see it's there in black and white.' I produce my order form with a triumphant flourish, shove it under his nose, and only just refrain from thumbing my nose and intoning, 'Na-na-ni-na-na.'

The delivery man looks at the form and then shows it to his sidekick. They exchange a look.

'Look, here's the old machine, disconnected, ready for you to pick up,' I continue.

'We can't take that love,' he replies with feigned patience.

'But why?' I fume, now ready to throttle him with my bare hands.

'Because that's a washing machine, and we delivered a dishwasher.'

I wait for the latest cloud of cement dust to settle, look at the box, and see the word DISHWASHER in thick black letters.

'Ah. Yes. So it is. Sorry about that. Thought you were delivering a washing machine,' I say feebly.

'No love, not unless you rinse your smalls in the dishwasher,' he roars with laughter at his own joke.

'Or chuck the dishes in the washing machine,' the other one adds, not to be outdone. They crease up.

I, on the other hand, red-faced with embarrassment, can only manage a feeble laugh and usher them out the door before they crack any more stupid jokes!

***

Choosing flooring is tricky, not to say time-consuming. So, to avoid taking up residence in the flooring shop, Dearly Beloved and I decide some samples would be useful. Sadly, the flooring shop doesn't have a small sample of the flooring we like, so we're stumped.

'That one will do,' DB says, totally brassed off with the whole decision-making palaver, but I'm not convinced.

I've spotted a possibility, which is displayed on a large panel in the window. 'We couldn't borrow that display panel, could we?' I ask sweetly. 'Just to check if it goes with the dining room table we've ordered.'

'What, really?' DB looks at me as if I've completely lost my marbles. 'It's huge!'

'That's fine, madam,' the long-suffering assistant quickly complies, probably desperate to get his life back.

He helpfully lifts the panel into the car, and off we go to Furniture Village, where the dining room table is on display.

Now, the shop assistant is a fairly hefty guy, so a 6-foot display panel causes him no problem, but it's a different story for us two weaklings when we discover it weighs a flaming ton!

We eventually wrestle it out of the car and struggle into the shop, carrying it like a stretcher with DB at one end and me at the other. Aware that we look like two ambulancemen who have lost their sanity, we're not surprised when a couple of customers look at us in amazement, obviously thinking, 'What on earth are these two half-wits doing!'

It's Sod's law that the dining room suites are on the first floor, and the lift is out of order—so with great difficulty, we heft it up the winding stairs. DB, unaware that the wretched thing is slipping out of my grasp, carries on regardless.

'Hold on,' I hiss, not wanting to attract any more attention than we've already done.

'Can't stop now,' he says, 'I've just got a head of steam up.'

I can't hold onto it anymore, and my end drops with a loud clunk!

'Sorry,' I say weakly to the gawping customers who had no idea a trip to the furniture shop could be so entertaining.

DB stops, and I manage to haul my end up, and then, thinking he is ready, I propel myself forward. This catches DB unaware and drives him up the stairs at a gallop.

'Wait!' he yells. 'I wasn't ready! I nearly broke my neck then!'

I get a fit of the giggles and stand there helpless with tears streaming down my face.

'It's not funny!' DB fumes, which cracks me up even more. 'Right, after three!'

Giving the Chuckle Brothers a run for their money with a bit of, 'To me. To you,' we reach the top of the stairs, red-faced and panting. We spot the table we've ordered and drop the panel on the floor beside it.

'I don't like it,' I say.

DB's response is unprintable.

***

So, the clouds of brick dust have cleared at last, and we have a new kitchen! Mind you, we could have built the Pyramids quicker, but we've learned a lot.

- A builder's day, for some unknown reason, begins at the crack of dawn and ends mid-afternoon.

- Builders can drink enough tea to float Moby Dick.

- Builders can also eat King Kong's body weight in biscuits.

- Hearing loud sucking of teeth and 'Ooh, this is a much bigger job than I expected' every five minutes does not auger well for the bank balance.

- Brick dust has paranormal qualities. It can walk upstairs. And get through closed doors. And sneakily hides until you've spent hours dusting before chucking itself over everything again.

- A fridge freezer in the middle of the hallway is surprisingly very convenient.

LET THERE BE LIGHT

So, I ask my Dearly Beloved to put up the new living room lights while I get on with the ironing. It isn't long before I hear some fruity language emanating from the top of the ladder.

'Having trouble?' I ask sweetly as I poke my head around the door.

'Stupid bloomin' system, this is!' he replies as, yet again, he drops the tiny little screw that's supposed to secure the light to the ceiling. 'That's the millionth time I've done that!'

I realise that telling him he's exaggerating might risk apoplexy, so keep schtum.

'Would you like a hand?' I ask. 'I'll hold the light while you tighten the screw.'

'Hummph,' he replies, reluctant to accept help from someone whom he regards (quite rightly) as a complete plank when it comes to DIY.

I get the step stool and climb on it, but as it's not high enough, I end up balanced precariously on tiptoe, with the other leg stretched out behind, like some pensioned-off ballerina.

'Plink!'

There goes the screw again.

'You've dropped it again,' I say, stating the obvious.

'That was you, you wobbled!'

'Didn't.

'Did.'

'Only a bit.'

'The trouble is I can't see,' he grumbles.

'That's because we've got no light,' I say helpfully.

No reply, just a murderous look.

'Get a torch and shine it on the light fitting; see if that helps.'

I do as I'm told. Now, I'm not only balancing on tiptoe, but I'm holding the light up with one hand and pointing the torch with the other. I feel like I'm playing a vertical version of Twister.

'Hold the light still,' I'm told.

'I'm trying!' I say.

'Extremely!' is the reply.

At last, after a few more futile attempts, the screw stays where it's put, and the light is up.

'I'm going to turn the electricity back on, so tell me if it works,' DB says and scurries off to the fuse box.

'Okay?' he yells from under the stairs.

'Yes, I'm fine,' I reply, thinking foolishly that he's concerned for my well-being.

'Not you! The light!'

'Yes, it looks nice,' I reply.

'For Pete's sake, I don't care what it looks like! Is it working?' he yells again.

There's nothing shining.

'No!' I yell back.

There are more muffled expletives, and DB emerges, slightly dusty.

'I don't believe it!' he says, outdoing even Victor Meldrew. He pulls the instructions from the box, which is in the kitchen, and pores over them, muttering, 'Done that. Done that. Tightened that. Screwed that. Switch it on again,' he shouts.

'Any luck?'

'No, still not working.' I shout back.

'Right, that's it! The stupid thing can go back to the shop,' he rages.

He strides into the living room ready to yank the offending light out of the ceiling by brute force, when he stops in his tracks.

'What the...!' He restrains himself in the nick of time, but his face clearly says, 'You complete idiot!'

'What?' I say, wondering what I've done now.

'You didn't put the bulb in it.'

I look up at the bulb-less light.

'Oh....Yeh.'

Don't think I'll be helping with the next DIY job!

MAN VERSUS MACHINE

(This occurred just after the new £1 coins were introduced.)

Go to Tunbridge Wells.

Park the car behind Sainsbury's.

Discover, I haven't got £2.80 change for the machine.

Try using a credit card.

The machine says, 'Transaction has been cancelled. '

Try the card again.

The machine says, 'Transaction has been cancelled. '

Get slightly narked.

Decide change is needed.

Go to Sainsbury's and buy some bananas.

Get two £2 coins in change.

Put them in the machine.

Machine says, 'Transaction has been cancelled'.

Put money in the machine again.

Machine says, 'Transaction has been cancelled'.

Begin to fume.

Realise the machine will only take the correct change.

Go to Sainsbury's and buy a paper.

302

Get four 20p coins in change.

Now have a £2 coin and 80 pence.

Put money in the machine.

The machine says, 'Transaction has been cancelled.'

Consider kicking the stuffing out of the machine.

Realise the machine doesn't like £2 coins.

Go to Sainsbury's.

Buy some milk.

Check-out girl greets me like an old friend.

Get two £1 pound coins.

Put money in the machine.

The machine says... 'Transaction has been SODDING CANCELLED.'

Realise pound coins are the new type, so the machine won't accept them.

Consider setting fire not only to the machine but the entire car park.

See, nice man. Throw myself at his feet.

Beg him for two £1 coins that are not the new type.

The man looks slightly scared at the gibbering female with murder in her eyes.

Gives me two £1.00 coins and beats a hasty retreat.

Fix the machine with a steely stare and insert coins.

.....................A ticket is issued.

Feel triumphant at finally beating the machine's dastardly plot.

Give it a sly kick anyway.

MAN'S BEST FRIEND?

We're dog-sitting at the moment for the son and heir who's gone in search of some welcome Portuguese sun. Brooke is a cute Red Fox Labrador puppy, so we are looking forward to idyllic morning walks by the river with Brooke frolicking around our feet, and passers-by stopping to marvel at the sweet-natured dog.

The first morning starts well. The river is sparkling in the early morning sunshine, there's no one to disturb the peace and Brooke is obligingly doing some frolicking. What we don't realise is that ensconced on the riverbank, half concealed behind a bush, is a fisherman.

There he sits on his flimsy collapsible chair, hat tipped over his eyes, just whiling away the time and enjoying the tranquillity of the riverbank. That is when we discover that Brooke has transitioned from an endearing puppy into a bolshie teenager.

'Oi you! Old geezer!' she barks. 'Wot you doin' sitting there! This is my patch, innit!''

With that, she launches herself at the poor, unsuspecting fisherman, who jumps out of his skin at this barking mutt heading straight for him. There is a horrible moment when his chair teeters dangerously on one leg, and I fear that he's going headfirst into the river, but a desperate last-minute

305

adjustment thankfully saves him from a dunking. I frantically pull Brooke back and apologise profusely.

'I'm so sorry,' I say, 'We're just training her.'

I can almost hear him say, 'Where? The Hound of the Baskervilles Finishing School?' as he cowers behind the bush.

I drag Brooke away, who is looking smug and metaphorically brushing off her paws while growling, 'Ave that, pal!'

Peace and harmony are restored, and we continue on the walk, but a little way down the path, I spot a flash of red in the distance. It's a jogger in a red T-shirt. I realise this is a 'get-her-on-the-lead-quick' situation, but too late—she's off like a hairy Exocet missile. The jogger does a swift, panicked jump to the left out of her trajectory, followed by a flurry of even more panicked jumps as he finds himself in a swathe of stinging nettles.

Brooke thinks this is great fun and joins in the game, jumping to the left and then to the right like a canine cast member of the Rocky Horror Show—all the time trapping the jogger in his nettle nightmare.

I eventually get her on the lead.

'Sorry,' I apologise, 'We're just tr....' but I'm cut short as he mutters something about dogs and their useless owners as he limps off on nettle-stung legs. I consider calling after him with the consoling fact that his legs now match his T-shirt but think better of it.

We continue the rest of our circuit, which passes uneventfully until we're almost back at the start. Suddenly, there's another flash of red in the distance. I have a horrible moment of *deja vu* and then realise that the jogger has been following the same circular path as us but in the opposite direction!

It becomes obvious that this is not so much 'red rag to a bull' as 'red T-shirt to a Labrador' because one glimpse is enough for Brooke to take on ballistic missile mode again. By the time we catch up with her, she's got the same unfortunate jogger pinned against a fence. He is now a veritable vision in red: red T-shirt, mottled red legs, and a puce face to match.

Brooke is back in moody adolescent mode, her bark as good as telling him, 'You ain't going nowhere, bruv!'

I drag her away, once more apologising profusely, but it's obvious the only way he'll be happy is if he organises Brooke, a one-way ticket to the vet.

We arrive home stressed to the eyeballs and dreading tomorrow morning when the whole fiasco could be repeated. Are treadmills for dogs a thing?

MISTAKEN IDENTITY

So, my Dearly Beloved and I are doing a bit of shopping at Tesco. As usual, he's disappeared with the trolley while I stagger around the shop with armfuls of tins, packets, and jars, like some human version of 'Buckaroo.'

I eventually catch a glimpse of DB and head over to where he is. My eyes are fixed on the trolley to see how many unnecessary 'bargains' he's put in there this time when I spot a packet of ready-prepared mashed potato.

'I mean, seriously? How much effort does it take to mash a bit of potato?' I think.

I pick it up, examine it suspiciously, and say, 'Eurgh! What's this? It looks disgusting!'

There is no response from DB.

'AND I bet it costs a fortune!'

Still no response.

'I mean, that's just laziness, buying that!'

DB still hasn't uttered a word, so I look up and come face to face with a complete stranger. It isn't DB at all! Heaven knows where DB is, but he's certainly not the man who's standing in front of me, the man whose mashed potato I have in my hand, the man who is completely flabbergasted by this ranting woman who has accosted his shopping trolley and swiped his mash.

To be fair, he's dressed like DB; blue jacket and brown jeans, but there the resemblance ends. This is definitely not MY man. This is a completely different man, a man whose mashed potato I have been rubbishing for the past two minutes!

I apologise profusely, 'I'm SO sorry. I thought you were my husband,' and carefully place the mashed potato back in his trolley.

'I might put that back,' he says meekly, obviously traumatised by my disparaging remarks.

'No, please don't. I'm sure it's lovely,' I say, then add, not very helpfully, 'It's probably nicer than it looks.'

'No, it's alright,' he says forlornly, 'I've gone off it now,' and he puts the mash back in the chiller and heads for the checkout.

Meanwhile, DB appears around the corner with a trolley laden with such useful items as 3 packs of bean sprouts for the price of 2. Great bargain if you like bean sprouts. We don't.

'Everything ok, dear?' he asks, sensing there's something wrong.

'Don't ask!' I say, not knowing where to begin.

Suffice it to say that I've been distraught all evening at the thought of some poor chap who is not only appalled by the prospect of visiting another supermarket—any supermarket—ever again, but who is now facing a dinner that's utterly 'mash-less.' Bangers and no mash. Shepherds and no pie. Bubble and no squeak.

Oh, the guilt!

MONDAY IS WASHING DAY

Those of you who are past the prime of life might remember the Scaffold hit, 'Monday is washing day. Is everybody happy? You bet your life we are.' Well, change the last line to, 'You bet your life we're NOT,' and you'll have some notion of what it was like in our kitchen last washing day.

All is going swimmingly (a prophetic word as it happens). My Dearly Beloved's smalls are churning around quite happily when suddenly the washing machine stops in mid-cycle.

'That's a bummer,' I think and proceed to twiddle dials and press buttons but to no avail. I summon DB. He twiddles, dials, and presses buttons, but nothing. Nada. Zippo.

'What do you think the problem is?' I ask.

'No idea,' he reluctantly concedes, hating to be bettered by a machine. 'Get the manual out.'

'It says here the drain pump could be blocked.'

'Told you it was that,' he says without a glimmer of shame. 'Great! That means the kick plate has to come off, and the door and we have to shift the bloomin' thing out of its housing, and my tools are in the garage, and it's snowing....' And he exits the kitchen muttering as he goes.

Ten minutes later, he reappears, slightly frostbitten and still muttering. 'Flaming freezing out there. Stupid thing couldn't break down in the summer, could it? Oh no, too much to ask....'

'Stop your mithering,' I say, 'and let's get this done.'

We both risk double hernias by hauling the heavy machine out of its tightly fitting space.

To make matters worse, what needs inspecting is at floor level, and as DB and I passed the spring chicken stage a while back, lying on the floor on our stomachs is no fun. I giggle that we look like two decrepit extras from Baywatch, minus the surfboards, but DB isn't in the mood.

As the machine is full of water, it has to be drained using a minuscule hose at the bottom. We, therefore, bank on only a minuscule amount of water escaping. Wrong. DB unplugs the stopper, water gushes everywhere, and we're soon in a scene from 'Titanic'.

'Quick! Grab something,' Leonardo yells as everything in close proximity is deluged.

I rush back with a bucket.

'No, that's too big!' he yells, getting wetter by the minute. 'Get something shallower.'

I rush back with a baking tray.

'No, that's too shallow!'

'Blimey, make your mind up!' I say huffily.

Meanwhile, DB tries to quell a rising dam of water with his thumb (think less 'Little Dutch Boy' and more 'Slightly Paunchy Kentish Man').

'Hurry up, she's gonna blow!' he shouts as if he's in a cut-price disaster movie.

The only suitable thing I can find is a small jug, which DB fills from the hose and then dispenses into a larger jug, which I have at the ready, before quickly jamming his jug under the hose again. Muggins' job is to haul herself to her feet from a squat and empty the large jug into the sink. And repeat. A lot. At top speed.

Now, imagine how many small jugfuls it takes to empty a full-sized washing machine, and you'll know how many squats I execute. A Joe Wicks workout is a cinch in comparison.

After the umpteenth trip, my knees have gone AWOL, and I'm staggering around the kitchen like I'm trolleyed. I try heading for the sink, but my wobbly knees have other ideas and keep taking me in a different direction.

DB spots this from his relatively comfortable position lying on the floor.

'Stop messing about!' he chastises, 'we'll never get this done!'

The phrase, 'Don't kick a man when he's down,' pops into my mind—but I'm sorely tempted.

At last, the machine is empty, all pipes have been checked and cleared of foreign objects, and hey presto!

Nothing.

I look at DB in despair.

'Wait a minute!' he says. 'I've just remembered something. I was talking to Dave, the plumber, the other week, and he said if the outside pipe of a washing machine gets frozen, it'll stop the machine from working!'

'Great,' I say, rubbing my arthritic knees, 'You couldn't have remembered that an hour ago before I needed two knee replacements. I may never walk again!'

'Bit dramatic, there, old girl,' he replies as he goes off to find the hairdryer.

Ten minutes later...success!

DB's boxers are freed from captivity and my new knee braces are ordered and in the post.

***

After the excitement of the Poseidon Adventure yesterday, I try cajoling DB to lag the outside pipe of the washing machine so the same problem won't recur, and I can finish off the washing from the day before.

'You realise it's -3 out there,' grumbles DB. 'I've only just defrosted from the trip to the garage yesterday.' Then adds triumphantly, 'And anyway, I've got nothing to lag it with.'

'What about that bit of useless polystyrene that's cluttered up the garage for years because "it'll come in handy one day"?' I remind him.

Outwitted, DB grabs his ice pick and crampons and unwillingly sets off for the garage.

He returns with a long polystyrene box thingummy, which we then try to tie round the pipe with string. I say 'try' advisedly, because tying string in thick ski gloves should definitely feature in the next Winter Olympics.

'Hold that end,' says DB as he fails to tie a knot for the umpteenth time.

I try to, but my gloves are so thick I can't tell if I've got hold of it or not. The end drops from my fingers just as DB gets his end at the ready.

'You're supposed to be holding it!'

'I was.'

'Well, clearly not, as you've just dropped it.'

We try again. Several times. The same thing happens.

'I've never known someone as ham-fisted!' complains DB.

'Well, you hold my end then!' I retort.

'Obviously, you haven't grasped the basic concept of a string-holding cooperative,' DB grumbles.

'I know what I'd like to grasp!' I think, eyeing up DB's throat.

I sense he's on the verge of a total paddy, so I persuade him that we both need to take off our gloves, but frozen fingertips are equally useless. A ten-minute job takes us half an hour. Every few minutes, we have to blow into our hands or beat our bodies like two demented, over-dressed sumo wrestlers.

At last, it's done—it's a bit naff t.b.h.—but we're too cold to care, so DB stomps off back inside to thaw out his extremities.

Pleased we've again solved the problem, I put in the next load of washing, set the programme, and..... nothing. Nada. Zippo.

Sound familiar?

I summon Barry Bucknall from the nice, warm living room.

'What now!' he exclaims.

'It hasn't worked,' I say. 'We need to defrost the pipe again!'

'No way!' DB states resolutely. 'It's going to take 'til July to thaw out my nether regions as it is!'

To avoid another dose of hypothermia, we try every combination of washing programmes to see if it will work, but it's futile.

There's nothing else for it; we don the polar outfits again, wrestle with the string again, blow hot air on the pipe again, tie on the lagging again, risk terminal frostbite again and rush back into the house to press the start button again. Nowt.

DB looks at the machine in defeat.

'Wait a minute.... what does that key symbol on the screen mean?'

'Don't know,' I say, 'I'll get the manual.'

I flick through the manual again and then stop in horror as I see the words, 'CHILD LOCK - MACHINE WON'T FUNCTION IF THIS IS SELECTED.'

Aaaargh!

During the all-in wrestling match we had with the machine yesterday to get it out of its housing and back again, we must have touched the child lock button!

I'm left with a dilemma: do I risk telling DB that dicing with death twice in Arctic conditions was totally unnecessary, or do we just never wash any clothes again?

Hygiene or Hanging—it's a tough choice.

PIPE DREAMS

We're in the House of Fraser. As usual, I've parked Dearly Beloved in the cafe while I do a bit of retail therapy. Now, one thing you don't expect in your local department store is to be assailed by a pipe band in full throttle, but for us Scots, there is nothing better than the 'skirl of the pipes' to warm your sporran, so I'm delighted. The pipers are all, shall we say, 'mature' gentlemen, but their enthusiasm would put any young whipper-snapper boy band to shame.

I'm looking at some new boots, tapping my foot in time with the music and contemplating whether they would like a slightly knackered Scottish dancer to join them, when Dearly Beloved rings me from the cafe.

'Can you hear that cacophony,' he says. 'It's blooming deafening.'

'Oi, that's my countrymen you're talking about,' I reprimand him. 'I was just thinking about giving them a touch of the Gay Gordons,' I add, feeling very patriotic.

'Can you say that these days?' DB asks.

I ignore him.

'On second thoughts, I'd better not,' I say, realising it's about a hundred years since I did any Scottish country dancing. 'I might pull something.'

'Probably an 80-year-old piper,' quips DB.

I hang up and continue to enjoy the music.

As the number finishes, the lead piper spots me and comes over for a chat. He introduces himself as Douglas and tells me with pride in his voice that he's 84 and has been a piper for over sixty years.

Now, you might not think he'd be a prime candidate to win my affections, what with being 84 and in possession of what becomes increasingly apparent, a set of wayward dentures, but it is love at first sight. Why? When I ask if he'd mind if I take a picture of them all, he turns to his fellow pipers and says, 'This wee lassie would like a picture....'

That's what did it—this wee lassie was in love.

STAR WARS

We're at the Royal Observatory, Greenwich, as a birthday treat for our eldest grandson, Zach. The planetarium show is about to start, so we settle into the comfy seats with reclining backs, which allow you to lay your head back to see the dome easily.

It is dark; it is warm, and the Astronomer giving the talk has a soothing voice. He tells us about the wonders of the universe, and we all sit in hushed amazement.

Well, I say all…

Suddenly, the silent wonderment is shattered for everyone by the most enormous SNORE, one which an elephant with nasal congestion couldn't surpass. Grandpa has fallen asleep. I dig him hard in the ribs in the hope he'll stop.

With a grunt and a mumbled, 'Whassamatter?' he opens his eyes, but I can tell it's only a token gesture. His eyes close, and in seconds, the snores start again, only louder. The audience reluctantly drag their attention from the awe of the planetary display above, to try to spot the eejit who is making all the racket. Zach is in fits of giggles while I, engulfed by embarrassment, look daggers at Rip Van Winkle—real ones if I could have laid hands on some. The look isn't working, so I employ a sharper dig and hiss, 'Wake up! You're snoring,' Grandpa reluctantly prises his eyes open.

'I'm just having forty winks,' he whispers. 'No one will know. It's dark.'

'The entire universe knows you're having forty winks,' I hiss back. 'You're snoring so loud it can be heard from outer space!'

'Don't exaggerate,' he protests. 'It wasn't that loud.'

'Let's just say, the Big Bang was a whimper in comparison! Don't you dare fall asleep again!'

Grandpa reluctantly hitches himself up in his seat and pretends to look interested through glassy eyes.

The Astronomer, now he can hear himself think, continues his commentary while I stand guard, ready to break a rib at the first sign of another soporific snort!

TEA FOR TWO

We're celebrating our 47th Anniversary with a swanky afternoon tea at Fortnum and Mason.

The tearoom is sumptuous, the spread is delicious, and the champagne is going down a treat. My Dearly Beloved is in seventh heaven as he's partial to a bit of cake and has donned his roomiest pair of trousers in anticipation.

We scoff the lot and are about to get the bill when the waitress appears with a second plate of pastries.

'Thank you,' I say, thinking she's made a mistake, 'but we've already had some.'

'Afternoon tea includes two plates of cakes, one each,' the waitress explains.

I can hardly believe my ears. We've already eaten enough to put Mr Kipling out of business, and she's offering us more!

'No, really...' I say, but I'm quickly interrupted by DB with a distinct look of panic in his eyes.

'I'm sure I can find room for a couple more,' he says as he grabs the plate from her hand before she can head back to the kitchen.

Eventually, we roll out of the tearoom to have a look at the food hall. There are so many goodies it's hard to choose, but we negotiate a second mortgage and treat ourselves to one or two items, which they put in one of their famous bags.

The weather is freezing, so we get a cab back to the station just in time to catch the train home. Suddenly, DB's face blanches.

'Where's the Fortnum and Mason bag?' he says in horror.

'I don't know, you had it,' I reply.

'Did I?' he says, feigning innocence.

'Yes, you did!'

'Are you sure?'

'Positive!'

'Must have left it in the taxi,' he says sheepishly.

Seeing my infuriated face, he continues swiftly, 'Don't worry, I'll go back to the taxi rank and see if the cab's still there.'

He scurries off double quick, which, for a man of his age, is no mean feat, let alone a man of his age full of cake!

The time to catch our train is rapidly approaching when, at last, he reappears, clutching the famous green bag.

'Hurry up!' I shout, 'We've only got a few minutes to spare.'

'Believe me, this is as quick as it gets!' puffs DB, now green around the gills as the threatened reappearance of two plates of cake becomes a distinct possibility.

'I've just had a near-death experience,' he explains, craving sympathy. 'I saw the bag on the back seat of the taxi, but this HUGE guy…must have weighed at least 30 stone,' he exaggerates for effect, 'was just about to get in, so I had to rugby tackle him….'

'Yeah, right!' I think.

'….and grab the bag before he drove off. He didn't like it.' He gulps nervously at the memory. 'He didn't like it one bit. Thought I was trying to steal his cab. Threatened to rearrange my features,' he gulps again.

'Blimey, what did you say?' I ask, almost feeling sorry for him.

'Just that if I hadn't rescued the bag, the 47 years of marriage I was celebrating was probably down the pan.'

'No, probably about it!' I say, ushering him onto the train.

THE ENIGMA OF SAT NAVS

We set off for a trip to Bletchley Park—home of the Enigma machine, code breakers, and spies. My very own 007 (the name's Beloved, Dearly Beloved) is excited. We punch the postcode into our clapped-out sat nav and set off.

It's not too long before it assures us, 'You have arrived at your destination.'

'Really?' I question as I look at the large building in front of us. 'Either Bletchley Park is cunningly disguised as a DIY store, or that is a B&Q car park.'

'Recalibrate the machine,' 007 commands, getting into the whole Enigma thing.

Miss Moneypenny does as she is told.

Some fifteen minutes later, 'You have arrived at your destination,' it says again.

'Obviously another clever ruse by MI5,' I say. 'This is Bletchley Hospital.'

'I know that!' DB says. 'You don't have to be a secret agent to notice a ten-foot-high sign!'

007 is beginning to look stirred and not a little shaken.

He takes a deep breath. 'Punch in the postcode again, Moneypenny,' he says calmly, trying to keep the whole James Bond savoir-faire thing going.

Once more, Miss Moneypenny acquiesces. We drive on for another couple of miles

'You have arrived at your destination.'

'Oh, for Pete's sake,' 007 explodes, as we pull up in front of Bletchley Railway Station. 'No wonder they only employed geniuses there—you needed to be a flaming mastermind to find it!'

Seeing that he is ready to punch 'The Living Daylights' out of the sat nav, I decide to 'Never say Never' and employ the '(Gold)finger' one more time to enter the postcode to the elusive code breaking centre.

Eventually, we see the 'Spectre' of Bletchley Park appear in the distance. Heaving a sigh of relief that we have finally cracked the code of our recalcitrant sat nav, we realise ruefully that there is not a chance in Hell that we will ever be employed by 'Her Majesty's Secret Service'. Better rip up those MI6 application forms!

THE MAN NEXT DOOR

DB and I are in London for the night, staying at The Tower Hotel in St Katherine's Dock. We arrive early afternoon, check into our 10th-floor room, and are about to head off for a late lunch when I discover one of the key cards is missing. We've only been here five minutes, so it can't be far.

I turn everything upside down and inside out, but nada. DB, meanwhile, is ensconced in the digital version of 'The Times'—so no help there then.

'I'll just walk back along the corridor to see if I've dropped it,' I say.

'Hunnnh,' DB replies, not lifting his eyes from his iPad.

I walk down the corridor, eyes peeled, but still nada. The only thing to do is return to the room and telephone reception.

I head back along the corridor to our room, 1052, and rap on the door. No response. I knock a little louder but still nothing.

Frustrated in the extreme that DB isn't answering because he's still got his head stuck in his flamin' iPad, I hammer loudly. The door is flung open, and there stands a complete stranger, not exactly dripping but definitely damp— obviously straight out of the shower.

'Argh, so sorry. Thought this was my room,' I apologise red-faced. 'I've lost my key, you see. Thought you were my husband, but obviously, you're not my husband,' I laugh feebly. 'Just thought my husband was in there, but he's not, so...' I trail off, seeing my long-winded explanation was doing nothing for this guy's blood pressure.

I knock on the next door down and am mightily relieved when DB answers, completely oblivious that his wife has just had an encounter with the slightly soggy guest in the adjacent room.

The next morning, we're up bright and breezy—apart from DB, who's had a bit of a rough night. This may or may not be something to do with his late-night snack of a prawn sandwich, which had been festering on the windowsill of an overheated room all day. Suffice to say, he's not really in the mood for breakfast. He's just in a mood.

We are shown to our table, and the waiter points out the breakfast buffet. We head for the array of cereals, and I decide to have some rice crispies.

Now, the problem is that, within the box, the cereal comes in tightly sealed packets. And if, like me, your rheumatic hands don't work very well, especially in the mornings, you won't be surprised to hear that try as I might, I can't open the packet.

DB, not at his sunniest, growls, 'Just give it a good yank.' I do as I'm told. The packet flies open, and a shower of rice crispies deposit themselves into the bowl of yoghurt that the chap standing next to me has just served himself. I turn to offer my abject apologies, and aaaargh! —it's the man from room 1052.

The quip, 'I hardly recognised you with your clothes on!' passes through my mind, but thankfully, good sense prevails.

Should I perhaps offer to fish out the rice crispies now turning to mush in his yoghurt? Or throw in the towel and just scarper? His face says it all. Scarper it is.

THE MYSTERIOUS CASE OF THE DISAPPEARING VICAR

It's Christmas morning and we decide to go to church. Now, there's a choice. We either go to our usual church, a twenty-mile journey away, or the village church, five minutes away. For DB, anxious that he might miss out on the Christmas brunch planned later that morning, the choice is simple. The village church it is, then.

The church is gently lit by flickering candlelight, and the hand-carved nativity scene takes centre stage. There are only seven of us, but we sit contentedly waiting for the service to start, drinking in the peace of the surroundings.

And we sit…And we sit…And we sit.

We've now drunk in so much peace we're positively inebriated!

The vicar is late, we think.

It must be held up in traffic, we think.

Perhaps he's had an accident, we think.

How can a vicar vanish into thin air, we think?

Have we fallen into a time warp and Christmas is next week, we think.

Whatever we're thinking, there is one inescapable factor. The vicar is missing!

Eventually, one of the congregation, who happens to be the churchwarden, comes to the front of the church and tells us that she fears the vicar, who is a temp or whatever a stand-in vicar is called.... Reserve Rev? Proxy Parson? Vicarious Vicar? Back up Bish? ... has had a senior moment. The poor chap is about 90 and only wheeled out at Christmas and Easter.

Anyway, it's clear that there's going to be no service unless we call on the good old British bulldog spirit.

The churchwarden, taking on the role of Capt Mainwaring, tells us to stand by our pews and await orders while we in the lesser ranks are variously thinking, 'Don't panic! We're doomed! They don't like it up 'em!' (well, perhaps not that last one!)

We're soon organised. The churchwarden takes the service, DB reads the Collect, and I read the Gospel. The other four just have to run around making the church look full.

All goes swimmingly until it doesn't. Not only is there no vicar, but there is also no organist. We could do with a handy kazoo or even a comb and paper at a push, but no-one can oblige, so the accompaniment to the carols is provided by a dusty CD of pre-recorded tracks unearthed somewhere from the back of the vestry.

Enjoying this unexpected ecclesiastical karaoke, we finish singing 'Hark the Herald' with gusto, and the track is switched off.

After some contemplative prayer, we prepare ourselves to sing 'Silent Night'. Sadly, unbeknown to the churchwarden, who is also multi-tasking as CD operative, the recording still had one verse left of 'Hark the Herald'. This now blasts out from the speaker at the same time as we belt out 'Silent Night'.

We look at each other aghast and obediently skip back to the last verse of 'Hark the Herald', but the churchwarden, realising the problem, has now fast-forwarded to the track for 'Silent Night',

So now we have some choices. Do we

a) soldier on with 'Hark the Herald'

b) abandon ship for 'Silent Night' or

c) break ranks, go AWOL, and find the nearest sherry and mince pie?

We keep calm and carry on, and by the end of the service, we're feeling proud that the good old Dunkirk Spirit has prevailed.

As for the whereabouts of the vicar? Who knows! Perhaps sunning himself on a SAGA cruise was more appealing. If so, let's hope he's signed up for the onboard lecture, 'Memory Tips for Seniors'.

THE RAIN IT RAINETH EVERY DAY (TWELFTH NIGHT)

We're here in not-so-sunny Stratford upon Avon for a few days. A visit to Anne Hathaway's cottage sounds interesting, so we pop into the Tourist Information office for a ticket.

'It's only a ten-minute drive,' the Tourist info lady says. And then she utters the dreaded words. 'Or you could take the footpath. It's a lovely walk.'

My Dearly Beloved's eyes light up. He loves a good walk. Me? I'm more of a 'let's go by car' kinda girl, especially if there are rain clouds on the horizon. That, plus the fact that going for a walk with DB never augurs well, so I'm a bit reluctant.

Tourist Info lady senses my hesitation. 'It's very picturesque,' she says. 'It'll take you through some lovely Shakespeare country, and it's only a mile or so.'

'Come on,' DB says, 'that sounds lovely.'

'But, the forecast says rain...... maybe we should take the car....' I protest feebly, but I'm speaking to thin air as DB has already set off.

So, the question is, should we have taken the car? Oh yes.

The tourist info lady obviously needs a refresher course on the highlights of Stratford as nothing resembling 'this sceptred isle', to quote Shakespeare, is to be seen. She's obviously 'avin' a larf', *not* to quote Shakespeare, as we find ourselves walking through a housing estate, then the back of a school, and finally a couple of scruffy allotments. And surprise, surprise, it starts to rain.

By the time we get to Anne Hathaway's place, I'm feeling a little damp, to say the least. With my head down against the driving rain, I'm so cheesed off I don't notice the ten-foot-deep puddle by the side of the road. Nor do I see the car, driven by Stratford's resident speed demon, zoom through said puddle, deluging me in a tidal wave of rainwater.

You would think that I could get no wetter, but it's not over yet. We squelch into the entrance of the cottage to meet what must be the only tour guide in England, hampered by a severe lisp. Unaware at first of the poor man's impediment, I stand facing him.

'Welcome!' he says. 'I want to give you the Thense of Thixteenth Thentury Thociety before Thtarting our tour.'

Well, that does it, as if the rain and the puddle haven't soaked me enough, this finishes the job!

I've had enough. Dripping wet, covered in spit, I go to find the tearoom.

'Never again,' I mutter. But then I said that last time.

***

Today's question is, is it raining as much as yesterday? Answer? Yes.

Am I getting as wet? Answer? Yes. Even without profuse puddles and lisping tourist guides!

Do I care? No.

Because here I am, at the Royal Shakespeare Company at last. It might have taken almost half a century since finishing at the Royal Scottish Academy of Music and Drama, but the 'has-been' thespian that I am, I can finally say I've appeared at the RSC!

Alright! It's only in a photograph taken outside (sigh)— but it's a start!

I stand there in front of that hallowed place where hundreds of our best actors have stood before me and begin to mentally brush up a couple of soliloquies. Well, you never know; rain can be treacherous. It makes surfaces very slippery. Slippery surfaces can be lethal. Who knows, one of the actors might 'accidentally' fall over and need an understudy. Not that I'd give them a push! I'd never do that! (Cue demonic laughter 😈 😈 Mwah, ha, ha!) And what a stroke of luck if I was there ready and willing to tread the boards for them!

'So, who would I play?' I muse out loud. 'A slightly jaded Juliet? A desperate Desdemona? A clapped-out Cleopatra?'

'Your best bet is one of the three witches,' DB says and then quickly dives out of harm's way.

Eventually, the rain gets the better of me; sadly, there's not a skidding actor in sight, and I'm forced to retreat to the bookshop and give up my 'dream......perchance to sleep....' Or was that the other way round?

***

We travelled home yesterday just in time to have a bank holiday Monday peacefully at home, away from the madness of holiday traffic chaos. So, ask me if I'm enjoying the peace and tranquillity. Well, I would be if we weren't driving *back* to Stratford on Avon. Yes, the same Stratford on Avon that we left only yesterday. So why are we driving back there so soon? Because my darling DB (said through very gritted teeth) discovered within ten minutes of arriving home that he'd left his messenger bag at the hotel.

So, this morning, we get up at 6.00 am. 6.00 AM! ON A BANK HOLIDAY! When any sane person is having a bit of a lie in and drive a 300-mile round trip to retrieve it.

'Hello,' says the receptionist handing us the bag, 'fancy seeing you again! When I said yesterday that we hoped to see you again, I didn't think it would be within 24 hours!' she laughs uproariously.

I manage only a feeble smile, too busy weighing up whether I should wait until we're outside before giving DB a hefty thwack with the pesky bag, or just do it here.

We set off for home—AGAIN. I think wistfully of other people's bank holiday—taking the opportunity to enjoy some local beauty spots or a lazy day in front of the fire with a good book, but not us. No, WE'RE enjoying the beauty spots of the M25 and the M40, the highlight being a loo stop at a service station. And imagine my joy when, only twenty miles from home, I see the words—HEAVY CONGESTION AHEAD.

So, if you should spot someone with slightly bulging eyes and a bag wrapped TIGHTLY around his neck, you'll know it is my Dearly Beloved. He won't be leaving it behind anywhere again. Not if I've got anything to do with it!!!!

THE SOUND OF MUSIC

My Dearly Beloved and I are in Canterbury, so we decide a mooch round the Cathedral would be nice.

I take a few photographs, and everything is hunky dory until I enter the Crypt, where I fail to see the sign which says in large letters—NO PHOTOGRAPHY. I'm just about to take another picture when a Cathedral Gruppenfuhrer spots me and hisses, 'No photographs!' Embarrassed, I fumble with my phone to shut down the camera and beat a hasty retreat back to the nave with my tail firmly between my legs.

I'm walking over to the shop which sells postcards when I hear one of my favourite pieces of music, Faure's 'In Paradisum', playing softly. Now, I hadn't noticed any music when I was walking around previously, but I think this is a lovely touch that enhances the spirituality of the place.

I choose a couple of postcards and say to the chap behind the counter, 'I love this music!'

'We don't usually have music playing in the cathedral,' he says, slightly tight-lipped.

'Oh, really?' I reply. 'Well, I think it's a lovely idea!'

The music continues.

'We think it could be a distraction,' he says, still sounding a bit miffed.

'Oh, I disagree,' I argue. 'Don't you think it enhances the atmosphere? Especially a soft and gentle piece like this. This is one is my favourites!'

He says nothing and is now looking thunderous.

Blimey, he's a misery! I think and quickly go to find DB to tell him about the grumpy staff that work here.

I find him waiting outside, and amazingly, considering I'm as deaf as a post in one ear, I can still hear the music playing.

'I can still hear that lovely music from the Cathedral,' I say.

'Of course you can, you dozy dingbat,' says DB. 'It's coming from your phone!'

That's when I realise that in my haste to switch off my camera in the Crypt, I must have touched the music app, which started to play!

Idiot.

Remembering my insistence to the outraged postcard seller that music in the cathedral was a wonderful idea, I cringe deeply. Can you imagine the conversation between him and the Cathedral Gruppen Fuhrer at tea break:

'I had a complete dimwit in the Crypt this morning— taking pictures despite the ruddy great sign saying no photographs!'

'Ha! That's nothing I had some nutter playing music, bold as brass!'

Yep. Don't think I'll be visiting the Cathedral again any time soon!

THE SWEET TREAT OF AUTUMN

It's a lovely day. The late autumn sun is shining from a clear blue sky.

'We should go to Sheffield Park to see the autumn colours,' I say to DB.

'Really?' he says, never being one to revel overmuch in the beauty of nature. 'What's there?'

I employ my best eye roll. 'Well, the clue's in the word "park".'

'So, trees.'

'Yes.'

'Just trees?' he says.

It's obvious he's not set on fire by the prospect, but I press on.

'Come on, it's a beautiful day; we'll take a packed lunch and have a walk; it will be lovely.'

He's still not convinced but brightens up when I remind him it's a chance to give his new car a decent run.

We punch in the postcode, but it turns out that Mildred, the sister of Doreen, the sat nav dominatrix who ruled the roost in our previous car, turns out to be just as bloody-minded about taking the longest route known to man when giving directions.

We've been driving for some time on narrow country roads when we reach a 'Road Closed' sign. Should we turn right or left? Who knows? We're stumped. We toss an imaginary coin and plump for the left, but Mildred is having none of it.

'Do a U-turn where possible,' she intones sweetly.

As there's not enough room in this country lane to turn a dinky toy, let alone a VW Tiguan, it's difficult to comply.

'Do a U-turn,' she repeats slightly more emphatically. We still ignore her.

'Recalculating,' she says with slight panic in her voice, but maths is obviously not one of her strong points, as the recalculation never happens. She's probably trying to programme herself to scream, 'FOR PETE'S SAKE, YOU MORONS, HOW MANY TIMES? DO A FLAMING U-TURN!' but she's been rendered speechless.

DB, as is his wont, continues to blithely ignore any sat nav instructions, convinced that gut instinct can outwit any satellite system with years of state-of-the-art technology behind it.

Needless to say, all of this has taken far longer than we intended, so as we drive up to the gates of Sheffield Park, it's well into the afternoon.

'Hurry up, I'm starving,' complains DB as he grabs the packed lunch and sets off to find a table. But it's as if

Mildred, in revenge for being ignored for the past 2 hours, has had a word with the Weather Gods because as we approach the tables outside the cafe, the sun disappears, and the temperature dips considerably. DB buys two steaming hot teas, and we sit huddled over them, like a couple of seasonally early Bob Cratchits, extracting what little warmth we can from them.

'I'm loving this,' says DB sarcastically as his teeth chatter. 'Nothing nicer than a picnic lunch in the freezing cold.'

I've just raised the last bite of sandwich to my mouth when he jumps up, brushes the crumbs from his hands, and strides off in the direction of the lake.

'Come on, it'll be dark soon,' he says. 'Let's get this walk over and done with.' He beetles off at the rate of knots while I'm left scampering behind him, trying to snap one beautiful vista after another like David Bailey on speed.

It's not long before dusk sets in. DB is peering dramatically into the gloom, muttering about the danger of crashing blindly into trees in the dark, so I suggest as a reward for his…. well, nothing really…that we have a hot chocolate before we make the journey home. His eyes light up, and he's the happiest he's been all day.

'With cream?' he asks.

'And marshmallows,' I say with extra enticement.

The hot chocolate arrives. 'Isn't that lovely,' I say, still in awe of the glorious colours of autumn that surround us.

'Fabulous,' he replies, surprisingly.

I'm stopped in my tracks. Has he been overwhelmed by the beauty of nature, after all, I wonder?

But no. It's his whipped cream, marshmallow-bedecked hot chocolate that elicits this response; for him, a sight far more alluring than any golden-hued foliage we've seen. Philistine!

'TIS THE SEASON TO BE MERRY...

So, the Christmas decorations are up, and once more, my Dearly Beloved has managed to wriggle out of it!

'Let's put up the tree today,' I say, as always imagining a lovely time of festive togetherness.

'Good idea,' replies DB.

He doesn't stir.

'"Let's" is the abbreviated version of "Let US." PLURAL!' I remind him, sounding as if I've resurrected my teaching career, but it falls on deaf ears. No change there, then.

The decorations are under the stairs, and somehow, over the last 12 months, everything Christmas-related has mysteriously migrated to the very back of the cupboard. So, I set to, to do battle with the rest of the junk so I can reach them.

'You couldn't give me a hand to get this lot out,' I shout from the depths of the cupboard.

'Sorry, what was that? Can't hear you,' DB says, suddenly afflicted by an onset of selective deafness.

I take a deep breath and try again. 'You couldn't......' then, realising it is futile, I give up.

On hands and knees, I begin to wage war on everything that lies in the path of the decorations. The first hazard is

345

near strangulation by a rampant Hoover lead, followed by the delight of a sharp dig in the ribs from the unyielding corner of a wicker picnic basket. And the highlight of the day? Kneeling on the upturned plug of a fan heater. Give me a stray piece of Lego any day!

Hearing the expletives emanating from the cupboard, DB decides to scarper and take refuge in the study.

The next two hours are spent with ME decorating the tree, ME trying to get stupid little sprigs of holly to stay where they're put, and, of course, ME facing the perennial wrestle with a set of bloody-minded fairy lights. At last, it's done. I go into the study.

'Looks nice, doesn't it?' I say to my Dearly Beloved.

'Yes, lovely,' he replies, his eyes not leaving the computer screen!

Irritated? Moi?

Let's just say if there had not already been a star on top of the tree, DB might well have been enjoying a new viewpoint!

***

We spent a lovely Christmas Day at our son and daughter-in-law's—delicious food and precious time spent with the family.

'I'll send Tam and Craig some flowers, just to say thank you,' I say to the Dearly Beloved, whose head is buried in The Times.

'Hmmm,' he replies, obviously not listening, which, after the Christmas decoration debacle, probably won't surprise you!

'It's lovely when someone surprises you with flowers,' I say somewhat pointedly.

'Hmmm,' he repeats, still engrossed in the latest headlines.

'Can't remember the last time I had some flowers,' I say winsomely.

Nothing. Nada. Not a dicky bird. Just a non-committal, 'Hmmm,' again.

Realising my heavy hints are falling on deaf ears, I give up and get on with ordering the flowers to be sent to Tam and Craig.

The following day, I'm in the kitchen when the doorbell rings.

'Someone's sent you some flowers,' DB shouts.

I run into the hall and there on the doorstep is a huge flower box.

'Aw, bless him!' I think excitedly. 'He WAS listening!'

I'm really touched and feel more than a bit guilty for thinking badly of him.

I look for the name of the sender on the box, just to be certain that they aren't from some unknown tall, dark, and handsome admirer who has been worshipping me from afar. Well, a girl can dream, can't she?

Sender: Mrs Fiona Bundell.

How can I have sent them to myself? I wonder.

Am I so frustrated at never getting flowers from my Dearly Beloved that I've done this subconsciously? What was I thinking!?

Then it dawns on me. Instead of filling in the recipient's address, I'd filled in my own!

Obviously, too much alcohol in the Christmas pud! Or perhaps just too much alcohol!

YES, DEAR READER, HE'S DONE IT AGAIN!

It's our wedding anniversary so we're spending the day in London. The plan is to go to the Wildlife Photographer of the Year exhibition at the Natural History Museum first and then on to the Goring Hotel for afternoon tea.

It's monsoon weather in London so we treat ourselves to a taxi from the station. The cab pulls up; I dash out and run up the stairs to the museum to avoid the rain, leaving DB to pay the cab driver.

I wait patiently to show the entry tickets when I hear DB calling my name. I turn to see him looking so sheepish that he wouldn't look out of place in a herd of Cheviots. Then I hear the familiar dreaded words.

'I've left my bag in the taxi!'

Marvellous. Trust DB to find a novel way to make our special day extra special.

Normally, I'm quite a phlegmatic sort of gal, but this isn't the first time we've had this drama, or the second, nor indeed the third! In fact, those of you who are reading these anecdotes may remember these previous incidents—so I'm seething!

'Ring the black cab lost property. Now!' I hiss at him. To say my teeth are gritted is an understatement. Think of a very stubborn crocodile with lockjaw.

349

DB, sensing my potential for imminent explosion, is somewhere between a shedload of Semtex and a second Chernobyl. He does as he's told, but there's no answer.

His bag contains his iPad, so we use the *Find My iPhone* app and watch impotently as his bag, nestled comfortably on the back seat of the taxi, enjoys a first-class tour of London's main tourist sights. All we can do is shrug, go and find a consoling cuppa, and get on with the day.

Fearing DB will somehow cause more chaos, I send him off to find a table while I queue up at the cafe to get the tea. I briefly wonder if I can persuade them to serve me a nice cup of hemlock or, better still, a large pot of strychnine, but English Breakfast is the best they can manage.

Lucky DB, is all I can say. Very lucky.

Printed in Great Britain
by Amazon

62543957R00203